7 INDISPENSABLE WORDS for EFFECTIVE PRAYERS

ELMER TOWNS

DESTINY IMAGE® PUBLISHERS, INC.
P.O. Box 310, Shippensburg, PA 17257-0310
"Promoting Inspired Lives."

This book and all other Destiny Image and Destiny Image Fiction books are available at Christian bookstores and distributors worldwide.

For more information on foreign distributors, call 717-532-3040.

Reach us on the Internet: www.destinyimage.com.

ISBN 13 TP: 978-0-7684-7596-8

ISBN 13 eBook: 978-0-7684-7597-5

For Worldwide Distribution, Printed in the U.S.A.

1 2 3 4 5 6 7 8 / 27 26 25 24 23

TABLE OF CONTENTS

Part Three

Part Four

Part Five

FOREWORD

IT'S all right to ask for big extraordinary things, but make sure the things for which you ask is God's will. Search your heart to make sure you are not asking for selfish reasons, or for your ease, riches, or glory (James 4:2-3). You must ask for things that are the will of God.

First, you must have confidence that your prayers are based on God's will. "This is confidence...that if we ask according to His will, He hears us, and we know when He hears us, we have the answer we seek of Him" (1 John 5:14-15, ELT). You find God's will in God's Word.

How do you know a request is God's will? It must be in accordance with Scriptures...it must glorify God... it must advance His work, i.e., His church.

Second, you must be careful not to ask for something that God has not promised in His Word. Jesus tells us, "If you abide in Me, and My words abide in you, you will ask what you desire, and it shall be done for you" (John 15:7).

According to this verse, there are three things that get your prayers answered: (1) you must be abiding in Jesus, which means you have yielded yourself to Him, (2) God's Word must control your thinking and asking, and (3) you must ask to receive. Therefore, your prayers will be answered when you ask for things promised in Scriptures.

Also, you must tie your requests to fasting and continual prayer. Jesus said, "...if you have faith...you will say to this mountain...move...and it will move...however, this kind does not go out except by prayer and fasting" (Matthew 17:20-21).

Can we really expect God to respond to our big requests if we don't invest a corresponding amount of time and energy in prayer? Just making a bold request doesn't always move mountains.

So, what must we do? We must make bold *faith requests* from the very depts of our beings. We must pray with all our hearts, giving up sleep for an all-night prayer meeting. We must fast and pray for a day, for a week, or for 40 days. We must sacrifice because we know God *can* answer and we must keep praying until God *does* answer.

A causal request rolling off our tongues doesn't move God; but God responds when we pray so diligently that we cry and weep. So, when is the last time you begged God for something?

Because we know God can answer, never quit praying. Keep praying even when everything seems bleak. A strong, bold *faith request* is not praying once and then moving on. No! When our faith tells us that the answer will come, we cannot quit. We ask for it when we get up in the morning and when we pray at a meal. We ask for it while driving around the city, and we ask for it right before we go to sleep. We keep praying, because we believe in a personal God who is guiding us to make extraordinary requests.

Finally, do not doubt in the dark what God has shown you in the light. The condition for answers is to, "not doubt in his heart, but believe...those things he says will be done" (Mark 11:23). You cannot work up confidence in the flesh. Neither does it come from circumstances. Confidence comes from God who has the ability to answer.

PART ONE

7 INDISPENSABLE WORDS
FOR EFFECTIVE PRAYER

Chapter 1

FORGIVENESS PRAYING

"We know that God doesn't listen to sinners,
but he is ready to hear those who worship him and do his will."

John 9:31, NLT

"Who may climb the mountain of the Lord? Who may stand in his holy place?
Only those whose hands and hearts are pure."

Psalm 24:3-4, NLT

"...and forgive us our sins, as we have forgiven those who sin against us."

Matthew 6:12, NLT

O F all the indispensable words you need to use to get your prayers answered, forgiveness of sin is first on the list. It comes from finding that sin that blocks any and all approaches to God. Your sins stand between you and God. Did you see the first verse listed above, "God doesn't listen to sinners" (John 9:31, NLT)?

Before you begin to pray, you must realize the holiness of God and that holiness is absolutely opposed to any and all sin. Then you must realize who you are—a sinner—who is offering a prayer to Him.

God is the Almighty Creator; He created the universes and this earth (Genesis 1:1). The universe contains trillions and trillions of burning stars, located in billions and billions of galaxies. The only thing bigger than the universe is God. He is unlimited in time (the sequence of events) and unlimited in space (the distance between objects).

But the greatest creative act of Elohim God was sculpturing the first human in His image and likeness. Can you understand that you—through a series of generations reaching back to Creation—came from Adam that first created being. Then woman was made from the side of Adam—not his head to rule over him, or his feet so he could trample over her—she was made by God to live with him, rule the earth with him, and she was his "helpmeet." Then Scriptures declare, "A man shall leave his father and mother and be joined to his wife, and they shall become one flesh" (Genesis 2:24). Then Adam exclaimed, "She is part of my own bone and flesh!" (Genesis 2:23, TLB). That first couple reproduced human children themselves into the population of the world. If that was their only influence, that would be wonderful. But they had another influence on mankind—sin. "When Adam sinned, sin entered the world. Adam's sin brought death, so death spread to everyone, for everyone sinned" (Romans 5:12, NLT).

Now, the problem is all people are born with a sin nature that makes them automatically sin. That means, "everyone has sinned" (Romans 3:23, NLT). What is so bad about that? "The wages of sin is death" (Romans 6:23, NLT).

Because of sin, "no one is righteous, no not one" (Romans 3:16, NLT). We are not good enough to approach God, nor are we good enough for God to hear our prayers.

But Jesus Christ, God's only begotten Son, was born sinless of a virgin, and lived His entire life pleasing to God—without sin (2 Corinthians 5:21; Hebrews 4:15; 1 Peter 3:22; 1 John 3:5). Jesus was crucified and in death, Jesus became our sin, our sin and its punishment was transferred to Him (2 Corinthians 5:21). Jesus died in our place. Thus, God the Father forgave our sins at Jesus' death.

But there is a second greater transfer. Jesus, righteousness (all Jesus was and did) was transferred to us at His death. "For God made Christ, who never sinned, to be the offering for our sin, so that we could be made right with God through Christ" (2 Corinthians 5:21).

So, God doesn't answer the prayers of sinners. God does not accept sinner in His presence, and sinners cannot approach God with petitions or prayers. Let's review what that means for you.

But you can come to God the Father through Jesus, because He said, "I am the way, the truth and the life, no one can come to the Father except through Me" (John 14:6, NLT). You can now come to the Father with your prayers. "If we are living in the light, as God is in the light, then we have fellowship with each other, and the blood of Jesus, his Son, cleanses us from all sin" (1 John 1:7).

But sometimes your prayers are not answered, and sometimes you slip and stumble as you walk in this dark world. "If we claim we have no sin, we are only fooling ourselves and not living in the truth. But if we confess our sins to him, he is faithful and just to forgive us our sins and to cleanse us from all wickedness" (1 John 1:8-9, NLT).

So, when you come to God in prayer, you need the indispensable ingredient of forgiveness. When you confess your sins you get two qualities, i.e., forgiveness and cleansing.

So, let's look again at the indispensable ingredient for praying, i.e., forgiveness. But continue reading in First John to see what God the Father says about your sin. "My dear children, I am writing this to you so that you will not sin. But if anyone does sin, we have an advocate who pleads our case before the Father. He is Jesus Christ, the one who is truly righteous"

(1 John 2:1, NLT). This verse tells us Jesus not only is the One securing our forgiveness, He also is our *Advocate*.

What is an advocate? An advocate is like a trial lawyer who represents your case and makes your petition before a judge. So, Jesus will speak to the Father for you to make sure your sins are forgiven. Every time you go before the Father to pray, Jesus will plead your case so that your sins are forgiven. He tells the Father you are justified. "Therefore, being justified by faith, we have peace with God through our Lord Jesus Christ" (Romans 5:1, KJV). That word *justified* means in lay terminology, "Just as if I had never sinned." God hears you because of Jesus telling the Father your sins are forgiven. That is why you pray in His name.

Jesus gave us only one prayer to present to the Father, *The Lord's Prayer*. It points to your need of forgiveness when you pray, "Forgive us our sins" (Matthew 6:12). Notice, this verse carries a condition, "As we have forgiven those who sin against us" (Matthew 6:12). Did you see you not only must be forgiven to approach God; you must have a *forgiving attitude* when you come to the Father for forgiveness. Being forgiven by Christ will influence you so deeply that you will develop a *forgiving attitude*. Just as God the Father forgave you, so now you forgive those who sin against you.

So, forgiveness gives you the ability to pray and get answer from God the Father. You not only want your sins forgiven; you want to develop a forgiving attitude toward others as you pray. So, two things. First your sins will have to be forgiven to be able to pray effectively. But second, you will need a *forgiving attitude* to pray effectively.

What is a forgiving attitude? It is lifestyle of living for others and help others and praying for others. But it is also living for Jesus, serving Jesus, and letting Jesus minister through you.

Chapter 2

PRAISE AND WORSHIP PRAYING

"But the time is coming—indeed it's here now—when true worshipers will worship the Father in spirit and in truth. The Father is looking for those who will worship him that way. For God is Spirit, so those who worship him must worship in spirit and in truth."

John 4:23-24, NLT

"Remember what it says: 'Today when you hear his voice, don't harden your hearts as Israel did when they rebelled.'"

Hebrews 3:15, NLT

I must admit that I found this a very difficult chapter to write, because I feel that I do not praise God nearly enough. Perhaps this is due in part to the feeling that I do not know how to praise Him rightly. Or perhaps it is because I have not been grateful enough for all that God has done for me. But I think the main reason that I don't give adequate praise to God is because I just don't know enough about Him. He's infinitely greater than anyone or anything I can think or conceive. My praise is so earthly—and God needs Heavenly praise. Any praise that I give to God is limited by my finite language and emotions. So how could I adequately praise an infinite God?

ANGELIC PRAISE

In my mind, the type of praise that God needs is of the Heavenly sort offered by angels. Now, when you think of angels, you probably picture beings dressed in white flowing robes with wings on their backs who fly here and there to deliver messages. Maybe you picture someone like the angel Gabriel who announced the birth of Christ to Mary (Luke 1:26-38), or the two figures in shinning garments that told Mary Magdalene and the other women that Christ had risen from the dead (Luke 24:4-7). However, the primary reason why angels were created was to give glory to God. "And one (angel) cried to another and said, 'Holy, holy, holy, is the LORD of hosts; the whole earth is full of His glory!" (Isaiah 6:3).

The praise that angels offer to God is far better than any praise that we as human beings can offer to God. For one thing, angels cannot sin, so their praise is not influenced by selfishness, duplicity, or any tendency to wander from God—in other words, angelic praise is not influenced by any of the earthly desires that hamper our worship. Angels worship God constantly, while we only do it now and then. Angels worship God with "God-speech," while we are stuck with the limitations and stumblings of our human speech. And angels also know more about God than we do, so they can praise God with better knowledge, better wisdom, and more exact understanding.

All of this brings up an important point. If God has a multitude of angels that can praise Him constantly with a form of worship that is purer and more Heavenly than anything we could possibly achieve, why does He need us to praise Him at all?

WHAT HUMANS WORSHIP?

In Psalm 103, David writes, "Bless the LORD, O my soul; and all that is within me, bless His holy name" (v. 1). So, from this we learn that we should praise God from the bottom of our hearts and with our very being. But notice the word "bless" in this verse. What does that mean? To bless someone means to *add value* to his or her life here on earth. We can bless people financially by giving them money, or materially by giving them something they need, or spiritually by giving them advice and counseling.

But how can we bless God? God doesn't need our money. He doesn't need any of the stuff we could give Him. He has all knowledge of His perfection, so there is nothing we could offer Him that He doesn't have. God needs absolutely nothing. So, how can we *bless* or *add value* to God? The answer is very simple. We can't. We can't do anything to make God more than what He is.

However, when we "bless the Lord" we give God something that He cannot give Himself. It is a bit frightening to think that there is something that God cannot do, but the truth is that God cannot worship or praise Himself. So, when we bless the Lord, we are adding the value to God that comes from redeemed souls who recognize His greatness and goodness for who He is and what He does for us.

When we praise God, we move out of ourselves and get closer to God than ever before. We move away from our prayers of petitions, *give us this day our daily bread*, and toward ones that focus solely on recognizing the glory and majesty of God. When we praise God, we do not ask Him to give us money, get us out of trouble, or provide us with anything. Our praise has nothing to do with us, but everything to do with God. When we praise God, we do nothing but offer our selfless devotion to God as we exalt Him simply because of who He is.

WHY PRAISE GOD?

So, why must we praise God? One reason is simply because we are commanded to do so. The writer of Hebrews says, "Let us continually offer the sacrifice of praise to God, that is, the fruit of our lips, giving thanks to His name" (Hebrews 3:15). Just as a grapevine gives forth the fruit of its grapes, so our mouth must give forth the fruit of our praise to God.

But another reason why we should praise God is what worshiping the Lord does for our hearts and minds. Each of us needs hope for something beyond ourselves. When we praise God for His infinite protection, we are lifted higher and closer to God's perfection than ever before. Praise is good for us because it keeps us from being pessimists. It keeps us from becoming bogged down in all the depressing circumstances of our everyday lives and focuses our attention on something greater than our present condition. Praise keeps us from being self-centered and negative.

Praise is also good for what it teaches us. When we learn to praise God, we quit being absorbed with ourselves and instead become absorbed with God. When we learn to quit praising our own efforts and focus on giving our praise to God—who alone *deserves* our praise—we begin to grow in grace and become more like Jesus Christ. And as we learn to do this more and more frequently, our relationship with God deepens. This is why the early disciples "were continually in the temple praising and blessing God" (Luke 24:53), and why Paul dedicated the Book of Ephesians "to the praise of the glory of His grace"(Ephesians 1:6).

Perhaps the greatest reason why we should praise God is that He *seeks* our praise and worship. As Jesus stated to the Samaritan woman at the well, "The Father is seeking such to worship Him" (John 4:23). We should praise God simply because He *seeks it*. God longs for us to long for Him.

We will never achieve the level of praise of that of the Heavenly angels when they worship the Lord. Yet we can pray as David prayed when he wrote, "Let the words of my mouth and the meditation of my heart be acceptable in Your sight, O LORD, my Strength and my Redeemer" (Psalm 19:14). And since we will never be able to praise God with the words of angels, perhaps we can praise God with the words of Scriptures. So, let us allow the Word of God (which is perfect), become our medium of praise. Let's use the Word of God so often that the words of Scriptures become our own.

SO, WHAT IS PRAISE?

When Jesus was in Bethany at the house of Simon the leper, a woman poured an alabaster box of ointment upon Jesus' head. She did it as an act of love and worship, and Jesus said that throughout the history of the church, her sacrifice would be recognized "as a memorial to her" (Matthew 26:13).

What happens when we attend memorial services such as the ones that are held each year on Veteran's Day or the ceremonies that are held to remember the events of September 11, 2001? What happens when we visit a site such as the Vietnam Memorial or the location where the Twin Towers fell in New York? Most likely, we remember what happened and adjust our lives accordingly—and often profoundly. So, when we read this story of the woman who gave all that she had to give, should we not remember all that Christ has done in our lives, and adjust our worship and praise to Him accordingly?

Of course, when the woman poured the ointment on Jesus' head, there were some in the room who complained. "To what purpose is this waste?" (Matthew 26:8, KJV). There will be people in this world who will view our praise to God in much the same way. They will wonder why we are wasting our time going to church to worship God, or spending time in prayer, or giving our money to the Lord, or even why we are wasting our energy to sing songs of worship to God. Maybe you have asked this same question, "To what purpose is this waste?" If so, hear the rebuke of Jesus. "Why do you trouble this woman for she has done a *good work* for Me" (v. 10, emphasis added).

So, what is praise? It is a *good work* that we pour out upon Jesus.

When we praise God, we take the focus off ourselves and put it where it belongs—on God. Think of some of the negative things that are happening in your life. Now, think about something that God did in each situation to help you through that particular problem. Did He send a friend with an encouraging word? Was there anything positive that you learned from the experience?

Make a list of all the things God has done for you, or just tell them audibly to God. When you thank God for all of these things, you begin to magnify Him. In Psalm 34:3, David tells us to "Magnify the LORD...and let us exalt His name together."

Consider the word *magnify* for a moment. Since it is impossible to magnify God because God cannot get bigger, what does it mean to magnify God? Well, think about people who wear reading glasses to see the small print of a newspaper. The glasses do not change the newspaper at all; they merely change the perception in the eye of the reader. In the same way, when we magnify the Lord, we do not make Him bigger, but rather we magnify the Lord in our eyes. When we truly magnify the Lord, we grow in our understanding of Him and grow as believers in Him.

You magnify God in such ways as praying Scriptures, singing hymns or praise choruses, or even giving of yourself in some ministry. Maybe you are not growing as a Christian because you have not learned to truly magnify God. The more you magnify God, the more you grow. Doesn't God need to get larger in your perspective?

David stated, "I will bless the LORD at all times; His praise shall continually be in my mouth" (Psalm 34:1). As you go through your day, consciously look for any blessings that God sends your way and pray your thanksgiving to Him. How will you make focusing on the blessings and praising Him throughout your day part of your routine?

Chapter 3

FAITH PRAYING

THE third indispensable word in answered prayer is *faith*. First, when you kneel to pray you look into the face of God and realize your sin is blocking your approach to Him. So, you seek forgiveness, entering a proper prayer relationship with God which is your first essential. Your second is to praise God for who He is and what He can do—He can answer your request. So, you worship Him for His power to do what you ask, and His mercy that moves Him to respond to us. Now what do you need? Faith in God's existence. Faith is God's power to answer. Faith that He will answer.

What is praying in faith? It is knowing that God can give you what you request, and confidence that God will answer, long before the answer comes.

In the winter of 1979, Jerry Falwell walked into the chapel of Liberty University and announced that he was cancelling the message for that day. "We're all going to walk up to those seven dormitory buildings on the hill that are half finished. We're going to see a miracle. We are going to ask God to send in five million dollars to complete construction."

Falwell explained that if any student did not want to get involved in today's prayer meeting, they could go get a cup of coffee or take a nap. But those who were with him would be part of miracle. As far as I know all 4,000 students joined in the long faith march up the hill to those seven half-finished dorms. We followed Jerry's instruction, "Walk around the buildings one time when you get there." He explained, "we don't have time to walk around seven times, like Joshua and the children of Israel walked around the city of Jericho. Today you won't see walls coming down, but walls going up." Then he said, "Kneel in groups of seven, and each one pray asking God for five million dollars."

As Falwell jumped from the platform to head for the door, I followed him. Ron Hawkins and Ed Dobson joined us. We marched up the street and around the buildings one time. Then we knelt in a group with seven Liberty administrators. I was the first to pray,

"Lord, five million dollars is more money than I've ever seen or touched. I don't have faith to ask you for five million dollars. That's more money than I can even dream of. Lord, I can't ask You for money, I ask You; give me faith to believe You for great things."

I didn't realize that television cameras were capturing what we prayed, and the following week I heard myself announce to the nation on television, "I don't have faith...Lord; I believe, help my unbelief."

Then the television zeroed in on Jerry Falwell who prayed, "Lord, You have a lot of money and I need some of it. I need five million dollars to finish these seven buildings, and I need it right away. When I get five million dollars, we can train eight hundred more young people who will be pastors, missionaries, lawyers, and teachers. Lord, I know You will send this money, so I will tell the contractor to get started tomorrow morning. Within a couple of weeks, I will need to make my first payment, so I trust You for enough money to come in right away for the first payment."

I listened to the confidence of Falwell's prayer and it blew me away. He really believed that the money was coming. I interviewed him for a story and began to dig deep, "Did you really believe the money was coming in?"

"Yes."

I went to his wife, Macel, and asked the same question, "Did Jerry really believe the money was coming in?"

"Yes."

To the amazement of all, the money came in and the dorms were finished, and an additional 800 students were added to Liberty University that year. God honored the prayer of faith.

Jerry answered me, "Didn't Jesus say that if we prayed in faith, He would give us what we ask?" He quoted, *"Therefore I say to you, whatever things you ask when you pray, believe that you receive them, and you will have them"* (Mark 11:24).

One of the foremost conditions for getting answers to prayer is to pray in faith. *"But without faith it is impossible to please Him, for he who comes to God must believe that He is, and that He is a rewarder of those who diligently seek Him"* (Heb. 11:6). Therefore, from this one verse we see two conditions of prayer. First, we must have absolute faith that God exists and hears us. Second, we must "diligently seek Him." God answers in response to our persistent faith.

PRAYING WITH BILLY GRAHAM FOR $35 MILLION

In 1998, I was a member of the planning committee for Billy Graham's gigantic project called *Amsterdam 2000*. Billy planned to bring together 10,000 evangelists from 235 nations of the earth. While most delegates were from the United States paid their own expenses, most from the mission field could not attend without significant subsidy. The conference must raise $35 million to pay their expenses to Amsterdam, Netherlands, including airfare, food, and accommodations for 10 days. To me that was an insurmountable goal, except for the intervention of God.

Billy Graham said, "I want to train them to do evangelism, just like I do it." Graham said that to the 16 of us on the planning commission through a televised conference hookup. John Corts, the Executive Director of the Billy Graham Evangelistic Association led our meeting. We were seeking to invite only evangelists who proclaim the good news of Christ, urging lost people to make a personal response to Jesus Christ and be incorporated as new believers into the local church fellowships.

Billy said, "My greatest legacy is not a school of evangelism with my name on it, but to have 10,000 evangelists doing soul winning the way I do evangelism, but doing it in their own native tongue within their cultural expressions of their native home."

Previously, Billy had organized *Amsterdam '83* for 3,000 participants and *Amsterdam '86* for another 6,000 itinerant evangelists. Each had cost $35 million. Now, 13 years later we were planning to train 10,000 more evangelists. There had been 13 years of inflation and many faithful had probably forgot about the great influence of those previous conference. But after skillful planning and careful budgeting that incorporated what was learned from previous mistakes and experience, the committee felt it could put on *Amsterdam 2000* for the same per person cost of $3,500, or $35 million for 10,000 participants.

I chocked at the amount because I am not a great man of faith.

I knew how hard it was to raise money—mass mailings, radio appeals, pledge cards, myriad phone calls, visits, and contacts, repeating the story, and asking for contributions. I thought to myself, "It is not easy to raise thirty-five million dollars. I have never seen Jerry Falwell go after that much money."

Then Billy said, "It will be easy." The opposite of what I thought.

"I will write and ask thirty-five thousand people to give me $1,000 each." He went on to explain, "There are about that many people who have over the years, each given $1,000 or more to the Billy Graham Evangelistic Association."

Then he added, "It will be as simple as writing a letter to 35,000 people and trusting God to touch their hearts and enable them to support the vision."

Then I impulsively raised my hand, "I will give the first $1,000."

What was insurmountable to me was a simple faith statement to Billy Graham. He believed God could supply millions of dollars because it included carrying out the call of God upon his life. Billy believed God could provide $35 million because it would lead to winning souls to Christ.

The money—$35 million—came in just as Billy suggested. The conference was bigger than anticipated. The foreign delegates flew into Amsterdam from all over the world—every country. Not only did Billy Graham pay all expense, Christian businessmen and Christian organizations gave each delegate a suit of clothing, a Christian library of books and other necessity items needed for ministry. I spent ten days as part of the teaching staff...watching God do miracles.

LET'S PRAY NOW

Great faith is not measured by your sincerity, your ability to believe, or anything within your heart. Whether you have great faith or weak faith, you can be used of God to pray and get answers. A man with strong muscles, and a man with weak muscles—barely able to move—can both switch on an electric light to illuminate a room. It's not the power of the man who throws the switch that determines if the lights will come on. No, not at all. It's the power of the generator that supplies the energy for the lights. It is not your faith that will answer your prayers...it is God Himself who answers prayers.

Once I complimented Jerry Falwell for his great faith, but he corrected me. "I don't have great faith; I have faith in a great God." The size of your God determines the answer to your prayers, not the size of your faith.

Jesus said, "*...if you have faith as a mustard seed...*" (Matt. 17:20). A mustard seed was so small that Jesus was saying, "If you have a little faith, as opposed to no faith—you could move mountains or God."

So how can you get more faith to become the one who can move God? Get a bigger God. First, learn about Him from Scripture. Second, read the stories of great heroes of the faith; get their vision of God. Third, rely on your God for answers, not on your ability to pray.

Remember, *"...all things are possible to him who believes"* (Mark 9:23).

Chapter 4

SURRENDER PRAYING

"Thy will be done."

Matthew 6:10

"Father, if you are willing, please take this cup of suffering away from me. Yet I want your will to be done, not mine."

Luke 22:42, NLT

"Then he said to the crowd, 'If any of you wants to be my follower, you must give up your own way, take up your cross daily, and follow me.'"

Luke 9:23, NLT

YIELDEDNESS is one of the keys to answered prayer. If God has not answered your prayer, then you ought to search your heart for there might be something that is unyielded to God.

Because sin is so deceptive, and we are spiritually blinded (2 Cor. 4:3-4), we need to pray for illumination that we might see any sin in our lives that we may not normally see. Paul prayed for the spiritual enlightenment of the Ephesians that *"the eyes of your understanding being enlightened; that you may know what is the hope of His calling, what are the riches of the glory of His inheritance in the saints, and what is the exceeding greatness of His power toward us who believe, according to the working of His mighty power"* (Eph. 1:18-19).

Some people are like Jonah, they refuse to do God's will; and they even run in the opposite direction. God must punish them as He did Jonah when a great fish swallowed him. It is only then that some will yield to God—as did Jonah—and only then do they go and do God's will.

So even before you begin to yield yourself to God, pray for spiritual illumination to see the areas that you are hiding from God. And in your prayer, you may find things hidden from you so that you don't realize there is danger in your heart.

There are many homeowners who have termites, but they never realize it until a pest inspection reveals a termite infestation is present. Then workers can apply chemicals to remove the termites. In the same way, we sometimes need an inspection by the Holy Spirit to find what in our hearts is keeping our prayers from being answered.

Paul tells us, *"Yield yourselves unto God, as those that are alive from the dead"* (Rom. 6:13, KJV). In the moment of spiritual yieldedness, we find life and peace.

INTIMACY ANSWERS

One of the most difficult answers to receive is when you pray to become more intimate with God. Note how John the Baptist prayed, *"He must increase, but I must decrease"* (John 3:30). Jesus said of all the men ever born, John the Baptist was the greatest, *"Among those born of women there has not risen one greater than John the Baptist"* (Matt. 11:11). Therefore, God must have answered his prayer for intimacy.

This means John the Baptist had more faith than Abraham, who is known for his faith. And John the Baptist had more courage than Elijah, who was the bold prophet. And John the Baptist had more wisdom than Solomon, who was the wisest of all men.

And John the Baptist had more intimacy with God than David who was a man after God's own heart. Simply put, John the Baptist was the most outstanding believer that ever walked this earth.

John the Baptist, who is the greatest spiritual giant of all time, tells us we need yieldedness to become more like Christ, *"He must increase, but I must decrease"* (John 3:30).

Can God answer your prayer, and you become the greatest Christian of all time? Can you become greater than John the Baptist? Notice how Jesus answered that question, *"But he who is least in the kingdom of heaven is greater than he* [John the Baptist]*"* (Matt. 11:11). So, yes! You *can* become the greatest Christian of all times. But the answer is not in giant Bible knowledge, or great preaching, or through personal evangelism, but the heart attitude by which you pray. The answer is yielding prayer, "I must decrease." You must surrender all to Jesus Christ. That's tough to ask, and tough to get. We are naturally throne-sitters; we want to be number one in life. We don't like to make God or anyone else number one—we like the power or glory of sitting on the throne of our life.

I've always been very slow to ask God for humility or patience because the Bible explains, *"The testing of your faith produces patience"* (James 1:3). I've felt if I prayed for patience, God would send me trials to make me more patient or more humble. But trials hurt and squeeze the joy out of life. Who wants misery? That's why I call this a difficult prayer.

Yes! The most difficult prayer in life is surrendering everything, or to decrease in any area of our lives. Why? Because at the very heart and core of each of us is a consuming desire to feed our ego—love me, protect me, exalt me, and accept me. It's hard for our inner self to yield our self.

Our passion cries out for love, or exhalation, or acceptance, or protection. So, is it hard to give it all up for God? We want more of the things that motivates worldly people...and more.

And all of us want to be number one; our great passion is to "exalt me." So, it's hard to pray for God to make us less important.

Then don't forget social acceptance we all desire, "accept me." We want to be one of the gang, so it's hard to pray for God to decrease our social acceptance.

And finally, we all desire "protect me;" we don't want anyone treading on our reputation or taking away our things or money. So, it's hard to give any of it up.

It seems *"me"* is at the core of everything I do. How can I pray for "me" to decrease? That's a hard prayer!

So why is yielding to God one of the most difficult prayers to make? Because giving up involves dying that Christ may live in us. Didn't Jesus say, *"Except a corn of wheat fall into the ground and die, it abideth alone: but if it die, it bringeth forth much fruit"* (John 12:24, KJV). When we learn to die to selfish things, we begin to live for God. But that's hard.

Paul reminded us that our spiritual death is a daily struggle when he said; *"I die daily"* (1 Cor. 15:31). None of us want to give up anything at any time; we fight and struggle to stay in control. So, the prayer of yielding is the most difficult of all prayers.

We love the world and we love to live our own lives at our own pace. Did you get that "you" and "I" are at the center? Everything in our earthy lives revolves around our selfish existence. When the world says, "watch out for number one," the Christian must realize that being number one may keep them from answered prayers.

How can we say "Jesus first" when our lives demand love me, exalt me, protect me, accept me?

LET'S PRAY NOW

Remember, this is praying for spiritual surrender. You can't do anything in the flesh to please God. You can't flog yourself to death, as did some medieval monks who tried to answer their own prayers with whips. You can't starve yourself to death, or isolate yourself to death, nothing like that.

When you yield everything to God—but most importantly—yield yourself to God, then He begins to answer your prayers.

Chapter 5

ASKING PRAYING

"Keep on asking, and you will receive what you ask for. Keep on seeking, and you will find. Keep on knocking, and the door will be opened to you. For everyone who asks, receives. Everyone who seeks, finds. And to everyone who knocks, the door will be opened."

Matthew 7:7-8, NLT

"You can ask for anything in my name, and I will do it, so that the Son can bring glory to the Father. Yes, ask me for anything in my name, and I will do it!"

John 14:13-14, NLT

"But if you remain in me and my words remain in you, you may ask for anything you want, and it will be granted!"

John 15:7, NLT

VERY early in Jesus' ministry, He said, "Ask, and it will be given to you; seek, and you will find; knock, and it will be opened to you. For everyone who asks receives, and he who seeks finds, and to him who knocks it will be opened" (Matthew 7:7-8).

This brings up an interesting question: Why does God want His children to ask Him for things? If He is an *all-knowing* God, wouldn't He already know our needs before we even ask? And doesn't the Bible teach,

"Your Father knows the things you have need of before you ask Him" (Matthew 6:8). So, what is the point? Actually, there are several good reasons why God wants us to ask for things in prayer.

Perhaps the primary reason has a lot to do with *trust*. Imagine for a moment that you are planning a birthday party for a relative. You are very busy and have a lot of details to handle—so many in fact, that you realize that you won't be able to get everything done in time. So, you decide to ask one of your friends to help you. Two friends are available: John, who is a bit of a slacker and not terribly good with responsibility; and Bill, who is very reliable and incredibly organized. Which friend do you ask? Well, this should be a no-brainer, you ask Bill because you trust in his abilities to get the job done.

In the same way, when we ask for something in prayer, we demonstrate our trust in God. When Jesus told His disciples that He would do whatever they asked in His name, He was introducing them to one of the most elementary forms of dependence upon God. When we have to ask something of God, it means that we are dependent upon Him for the answers we need. It is another way of saying that we trust Him.

A second reason that we should ask is because God likes to be asked. If you are a mother or a father, don't you enjoy it when your children ask you for things? Sure, you probably already know what your kids need, but it is still a good feeling to know they depend on you to provide for them. Parents who love their children also want them to love them back. Asking for something is the most elementary form of dependence, and love grows in an atmosphere of asking and receiving.

Asking God for things in prayer also puts us into a partnership with our Heavenly Father. If we share an office with someone, we have to work with one another, share tasks, and rely on each other for support. We have to ask for what we need and then receive those things from the other person. In the same way, we are coworkers with God in bringing His Kingdom to the earth. "For we are God's fellow workers; you are God's field, you are God's building" (1 Corinthians 3:9). When we partner with God in His great task, it makes our "asking" even greater.

Of course, this also means that asking for things enriches our fellowship with God. When we tell God what is on our heart and ask for His help, our relationship with our Heavenly Father is deepened. We learn to rely on God for strength, and when He answers our prayers, it bolters our faith in Him. God is pleased when we share things of great importance.

But when we say, "I will not bother God with these minor details," doesn't that imply that we are questioning our relationship with Him? Would we worry about asking a close friend for something that was of importance to us, even if we considered it something minor? Of course not, if we are truly close friends, we would know that the other person would want to help us, no matter how small or insignificant the request. We cannot hide anything from God anyway, so why try? It just ruins our relationship with Him.

What if we just kept our prayers on the lofty heights of praise, adoration, and worship all the time? What if we never shared our problems with God? What if we felt as if we could never ask anything from Him? Would we be acting honestly toward Him? And if we are not being honest with Him regarding our needs, could we honestly be worshiping Him? When we pray and ask God for His help, isn't that evidence of a healthy relationship?

Asking is a rule of the kingdom. It is the way that small children relate to their parents, and it is the way that God's children should relate to Him. Asking is not a lower form of prayer, nor is it an unsophisticated form of praying. Like breathing air, asking is necessary in order to continue our spiritual walk with God.

1. *Your prayers are answered when you obey God.* God is our Heavenly Father and He loves His children. We can go to Him just like a child who asks things of his earthly father.

A little boy often went to see his dad at the hardware store and each time asked for a nickel to buy a cold drink from the machine in the supply room. When Dad was angry, he didn't get the nickel. The little boy was careful to stay on Dad's good side when he wanted a cold drink.

"And whatsoever we ask, we receive of him, because we keep his commandments, and do those things that are pleasing in his sight" (I John 3:22). Note that we get *whatsoever we ask* when we keep His commandments and please Him.

A teenage son asked to borrow his father's car for a date. He felt the family car was more luxurious than his.

"No!" was the answer. The father said, "The other day I asked you to wash my car and sweep out the sand, but you didn't have time." Within 30 minutes the boy was back to tell his father he had washed the car clean, and again asked to borrow it.

The Christian who disobeys God doesn't have the freedom to pray to his Heavenly Father and get the answers he seeks, without first seeking forgiveness. See chapter one, forgiveness is the first criteria for effective praying to get answers.

"Confess your faults one to another, and pray one for another, that ye may be healed. The effectual fervent prayer of a righteous man availeth much" (James 5:16, KJV). The phrase *availeth much* means "makes tremendous things available." When you are right with God, your prayers make the greatest things in the world available.

2. *Your prayers are answered when you get rid of known sin.* The Bible teaches that our sin makes it impossible for God to hear us. "If I regard iniquity in my heart, the Lord will not hear me" (Psalm 66:18).

Iniquity is sin, doing the exact opposite of God's will. If God tells us not to take His name in vain and we do, how can we ask Him to answer our prayers?

There is another verse that says we plug up God's ears. "Behold, the Lord's hand is not shortened, that it cannot save; neither his ear heavy, that it cannot hear but your iniquities have separated between you and your God, and your sins have hidden his face from you, that he will not hear" (Isaiah 59:1-2). God has the ability to help us and His ears can hear us, but our sin makes it impossible.

Robert was a mischievous boy. When his mother was angry, he hid in his favorite hiding place, a dark closet, where she couldn't see or hear him. When Robert was hiding it was not the time to ask his mother for money to go to the store for ice cream. If you have sin in your life, get rid of it; then ask God for your petition. Only then can you get answers to prayer.

3. *Your prayers are answered when you abide in Christ.* Jesus promised, "If ye abide in me, and my words abide in you, ye shall ask what ye will, and it shall be done unto you" (John 15:7). The word *abide* means to join yourself to God without any obstruction. It does not mean to hang on to God. When a branch is just hanging, on to the vine, it usually withers. But when the branch is growing from the vine, the life of the vine was flowing into the branch. Then it prospered and had fruit.

Just as the branch allows the life-giving sap to flow through it, the Christian who abides in Christ and His Word is a part of Christ's life, allows the Holy Spirit to control him. Usually we allow important people to do most of the talking and we ask them only pertinent questions. Likewise, when we give God the priority to speak to our heart through the Bible, we are prepared to ask the right request.

4. *Your prayers are answered when you ask according to His will.* God has a will which is His desire

for us. It is God's will that we pray for the things He wants us to have.

As a young boy, I always looked forward to a visit from my Uncle Herman who usually brought candy. But I had to ask for it. Sometimes he wanted me to rummage through his pockets to find the candy. It gave Uncle Herman as much happiness to provide candy as it did for me to find it. "And this is the confidence that we have in him, that, if we ask any thing according to his will, he heareth us: and if we know that he hear us, whatsoever we ask, we know that we have the petitions that we desired of him" (I John 5:14-15).

We must pray according to God's will. Once I prayed outside of God's will. While going through a Christian college, I prayed for money. There was a hole-in-one contest at a nearby golf course. Every person who hit the ball in the cup got $200. 1 prayed that God would help me make a hole-in-one, I needed $200. I knelt on the golf tee and asked God to guide my swing. None of the balls went into the cup. This was not God's way of providing for my financial needs. There was an element of gambling in the contest. Also, I used to enjoy playing golf and wanted some glory for getting a hole-in-one. God did not answer that selfish request (James 4:2-3).

How can you know if the things you ask are His will? Certain things are obviously God's will, such as people being saved. God wants everyone to be saved (2 Peter 3:9). It is not God's nature to frustrate His children; however, we may have to go through several doors, or stages of prayer to arrive at an answer to prayer. God may test our sincerity. We need to go through each open door as it appears. It may take a while to get an answer to prayer, but we should pray with confidence. Our Heavenly Father doesn't play games with us, hiding His will like an Easter egg. No, God gives us simple instructions to ask Him for the things we need.

5. *Your prayers are answered when you ask in faith.* Faith is expecting an answer to your prayer because

you have asked according to Scriptures, and your request in writing the will of God. As a schoolboy I sent coupons off for magic rings, code books and other trinkets. Every day I'd ask the mailman, "Did it come today?"

"Not today," the Postman would say. "Maybe tomorrow" I'd get so excited I could hardly wait for the postman to come. I use this illustration to show the attitude we ought to have when we are waiting for God to answer our prayers.

When we pray, we can believe that the answer is coming. "Therefore, I say unto you, 'What things soever ye desire, when ye pray, believe that ye receive them, and ye shall have them'" (Mark 11:24, KJV). The effectiveness of our faith determines the answers we get. "He that cometh to God must believe that he is, and that he is a rewarder of them that diligently seek him" (Hebrews 11:6).

When I was a child, I asked my mother for a quarter to go downtown. Twenty-five cents paid for the streetcar, popcorn, and a cold drink. I never asked for a dollar because I knew she wouldn't give it. I asked for what I felt she would give me—twenty-five cents. "But let him ask in faith, nothing wavering. For he that wavereth is like a wave of the sea driven with the wind and tossed" (James 1:6).

It's obvious some of us need more faith, not more time in prayer. Therefore, we ask, *How do we get more faith?* One way is to pray for it. Faith is sending off the coupon, but then going to the mailbox every day looking for the answer. Expect answers from God. Build yourself a spiritual mailbox. "I got a reply this morning," You will tell your friends.

6. *Your prayers are answered when your motives are right.* When we come to God in prayer, our desires must be pure. The Bible tells us that we sometimes do not get answers because of our lusts (selfish desires). "Ye ask, and receive not, because ye ask amiss, that ye may consume it upon your lusts" (James 4:3).

After salvation, I immediately began praying for a car. I had been poor all my life. I was in Bible college and believed I needed a car. "Dear God, give me a car," I prayed sincerely, then added, "If you give me a car, I'll pick up people and take them to church." I was bargaining with God. However, God looked through my words and saw my selfish desire. I wanted a car to take girls on dates and to impress my buddies. God didn't answer the request.

Two years later, I became a student pastor and still didn't have a car. I made my pastoral calls on a bicycle. In God's time, the members of the church got together to buy me a car. When your motives are right and you are willing to do anything to accomplish God's will, God will give you a car or whatever you need—in His own time.

7. *Your prayers are answered when you live peaceably with your mate.* Some husbands and wives fight. The Bible commands that husband and wife must live together peacefully so that their prayers can be answered. "Likewise, ye husbands, dwell with them according to knowledge, giving honor unto the wife, as unto the weaker vessel, and as being heirs together of the grace of life; that your prayers be not hindered" (I Peter 3:7). When a husband argues constantly with his wife, how can the children see Christ in their father? Then, if the father and mother pray for their child to be saved, their arguments have made it impossible for their prayer to be heard.

Chapter 6

PERSISTENT PRAYERS

"Rejoice always, pray without ceasing, in everything give thanks;
for this is the will of God in Christ Jesus for you."

1 Thessalonians 5:16-18

WHEN the Early Church was first established, the members, "Continuing daily with one accord in the temple...ate their food with gladness and simplicity of heart, praising God and having favor with all the people" (Acts 2:46-47). Did you see the word continuing?

On several occasions, Paul instructed believers to pray constantly. To the Romans, Paul wrote, "Be glad for all God is planning for you. Be patient in trouble, and prayerful always" (Romans 12:12, TLB). To the Ephesians, Paul wrote, "Pray at all times and on every occasion in the power of the Holy Spirit" (Ephesians 6:18, NLT). To the Colossians, Paul exhorted, "Devote yourselves to prayer with an alert mind and a thankful heart" (Colossians 4:2, NLT). And to the Philippians, Paul wrote, "Don't worry about anything, instead, pray about everything" (Philippians 4:6, NLT). But Paul was not alone in exhorting Christians to be in constant prayer. Jesus told His disciples, "Men ought always to pray, and not to faint" (Luke 18:1, KJV).

So, certainly *persistent prayer* is an important principle in the Bible. But what does "pray continually" really mean? Does it mean that we are to intercede constantly in the presence of God? If that is true, it would not leave much time for us to talk with our spouses, teach our children, or perform our duties in the work world.

PRAY WITHOUT CEASING

Some people suggest that praying without ceasing doesn't necessarily mean that we have to pray all of the time but that we should remain in the "spirit" of prayer. It is kind of like the churchgoer who remains in a constant state of reverence when they are inside the sanctuary...continually quiet and serene. Again, this does not leave much time for having fun with our kids, cheering at a sporting event or fellowshipping with our friends.

Perhaps it would be helpful to look more closely at the phase "pray without ceasing." The Greek phrase "without ceasing" does not mean "without stopping;" rather it means "intermittently."

My wife recently bought a new car with an intermittent speed for the windshield wipers. When the rain is falling in a light mist, the wipers turn on automatically to clear the windshield at a slow pace. However, when the rain is pouring down, the wipers rapidly swish back and forth to enable my wife to see through the sheets of rain. In the same way, we are to pray *intermittently*. Sometimes we will pray lightly and softly, as when the mist is falling from the sky. But at other times our prayers will rush out of our heart in a rapid and frenzied manner, as when a heavy rain is pouring down.

Perhaps a better illustration would be the crying habits of a newborn infant. When something bothers a baby, they cry heavily and continuously. But a baby does not cry unless they are hungry, wet, or need love and attention. In other words, the baby cries according to their needs at the time. In the same manner, we are to pray intermittently according to our needs.

Yet there is another point to consider regarding continual prayer. In Romans 8:16, Paul states that "the Spirit Himself bears witness with our spirit that we are children of God." A little future on in the same chapter Paul writes:

And the Holy Spirit helps us in our weakness. For example, we don't know what God wants us to pray for. But the Holy Spirit prays for us with groanings that cannot be expressed in words. And the Father who knows all hearts knows what the Spirit is saying, for the Spirit pleads for us believers in harmony with God's own will (Romans 8:26-27, NLT).

Whether we realize it or not, prayer is going on continually in us through the indwelling of the Holy Spirit. This works a bit like the electricity in our homes. We do not have power until we plug in our appliances to the wall outlet; but once we do, the power is instantly available for us to cook our food, warm our room, or crank up our stereo. In the same way, the Holy Spirit dwells within us and constantly prays for us, and at any moment we can plug ourselves into His constant stream of prayer—at whatever level meets our needs.

I cannot tell you that I constantly pray or even that I am continually in the spirit of prayer. But I am frequently amazed at just how much I do pray throughout the day. Quite often, I find myself praying while I am driving, I find myself praying while I am waiting in line or when I am between duties at Liberty University. Almost always when a student asks me a question in class, I pray for wisdom so that I might give them the right answer.

When I "pray without ceasing," I am not sure whether I am grabbing hold of prayer or whether prayer is grabbing hold of me. I just know that it works when I constantly yield to the Holy Spirit.

PRAY FOR THE LITTLE THINGS

Most of us live in a dichotomy. We have big spiritual projects for which we earnestly pray and seek God's intervention, but we ignore the humdrum of minutia. We pray, fast, and beg God to move the mountains that block our way, but we ignore the little pebbles scattered in our paths. What is the result? We see little connection between the little things in life and our spiritual walk with God.

Praying continually means talking to God about every aspect of our life—including the little things that we may think are unimportant to God. Many of us think that these little details have no connection to spirituality, but that is a wrong assumption. It is the small pebbles that get into our shoes that make it impossible for us to climb over the mountains. It is the small pebbles that accumulate and grow until they form the mountains that block our progress. There is a well-known saying that states "the devil is in the details," but the truth is that God is in the details. He works His will through the little things in life.

Consider the way that the Son of God entered into this world. God only had one Son, yet Jesus certainly did not enter the world in a *big* way. He was born in a little-known town called Bethlehem and in a little expected place—a stable. He was born to parents who were obscure on the world's stage and unknown to anyone outside of their little village—parents who were travelers on a voter's registration roundup (Luke 2:1-7).

When the Son of God was born, an angel of the Lord appeared to a group of shepherds in the nearby fields and told them that the promised Messiah had been born. To find the Savior, the angel told the shepherds to look for two small details. "You will find (1) the Babe wrapped in swaddling clothes, (2) lying in a manger" (Luke 2:12). The shepherds were not directed to a spectacular palace, the baby didn't shine with a holy radiance (as Jesus later did on the Mount of Transfiguration), there were no Heavenly spotlights to point out the child. The identification marks were almost imperceptible to the uninstructed eye. God's Son would be wrapped in strips of cloth; lying in a feeding trough. How is that for *minute details*!

But isn't this the way that each of us truly discover God? Just as the shepherds found Christ in the ordinary rudiments of life, don't we also discover God hidden in the minutia of life? Most of us just don't see God when we use our cell phones, grab a quick hamburger, or fill the car with gas. We go through life ignoring the reverence of God in the little things in life. But the truth is that if we cannot see God in the mundane routines of our daily lives, we probably won't be able to see Him in the big celebrations or when the spotlight shines on us.

We need to get away from the idea that prayer is some ecclesiastical experience where we contemplate the abstract and realize that the true function of prayer is to bring us into a continual relationship with God. We need to see God in our mundane routines, because when we do, things such as stapling reports, cleaning the kitchen counters, or buying groceries becomes a spiritual experience instead of boring drudgery. The difference begins in our perception and expectation. And isn't all life about perception and expectation?

PRACTICING GOD'S PRESENCE

When I was a freshman at Columbia Bible College, I once heard a chapel speaker talk about Brother Lawrence, a 17th century French monk who served in a monastery. The chapel speaker described how Brother Lawrence actually "practiced the presence of God" by continually practicing God's presence while he was washing pots and pans in his monastery's kitchen.

The possibility of sensing God's presence wherever I went made a profound influence on my life. So, I followed the example of Brother Lawrence. Even when I am caught up in the hustle and bustle of life, I have a private sanctuary in my heart into which I retreat. In my own little private sanctuary, I can practice the presence of God when I am sitting in a boring committee meeting or when I am caught in traffic gridlock. When I walk through the crowds on campus, I can experience the presence of Christ that is just as real as if I had slipped into a secluded sanctuary in which the presence of God is most evidently felt.

In my own experience, I have found that it is much easier to practice the presence of God when I begin my day by consciously spending time with God in prayer. My commitment to be there with God activates a strong discipline within me to focus my mind on God. But just setting the time aside isn't enough—I know that to truly experience the presence of God, I must barricade myself against thinking about business activities or all the things I plan to do that day. It takes energy to meet God, and it only occurs as a result of a dedicated will to make it happen.

But there is a second step beyond discipline. For once we make the decision to seek God's presence, we begin to develop intimacy through regular association with God. We soon find that we desire to develop a habit of practicing God's presence in our life. Just as a person develops a taste for a certain food, we develop a spiritual hunger for God.

So, what is *praying without ceasing*? It is developing *holy habits* to make our prayer life easier. Well, easier may not be the correct word—maybe it is making prayer more spontaneous or more natural. And in the process, we also make our godliness more practical.

come with a single experience but will grow naturally in our heart. A growing vine needs the energy of sunshine, the nurture of good soil, and the intermittent refreshment of rain. Unceasing prayer also needs energy, nurture, and refreshment, but most important, it needs discipline.

A girl who is learning the rudiments of playing the piano undoubtedly understands that it will take years of practice before her fingers will dance over the piano keys. But if she sticks with it and maintains good discipline, that girl—when an adult—will be able to play from deep within her heart. It will be a true art form. In the same way, discipline in prayer is key—we can know all about prayer, but the only way to develop unceasing prayer is to constantly practice it.

Constant prayer is not something that can be *taught*, rather it is something to be *caught*. No one can teach us how to talk to God—it is developed from our intimate relationship with Him and our commitment to meet with Him each day. As God shows us how to live, we talk to Him. As God shows us what not to do, we talk to Him. As we face the constant needs and difficulties in life, we talk to Him.

By continually talking with God—even if it is just a few sentences at a time—we learn that God can be intimate and personal. And through this constant communication—continual prayer—the relationship and intimacy between us and our Heavenly Father grows.

A CONTINUAL RELATIONSHIP WITH GOD

Just as a vine grows naturally and steadily up the garden wall, our ability to pray unceasingly won't

Chapter 7

GRATITUDE PRAYING

"Give thanks to the Lord, for He is good!"

Psalm 106:1, NKJV

GRATITUDE praying is the overarching theme of the Book of Psalms, which is praise, giving thanks to God. In essence, *gratitude praying,* or *thanksgiving praying* is the last of the indispensable influences in this book that leads to effective praying. What is thanksgiving indispensable? It is last, because gratitude is a mirror that reflects back on all you are as a child of God and is the acid test of your character, i.e., you walk with God. It is the essence of the first six conditions that lead to answered prayer, meaning that you cannot be a well-rounded Christian without being grateful to God for all He has done for you.

Remember, prayer is an essential relationship with God. You must be grateful to God and you give Him thanks for all He is and for all He has done for you. Because gratitude mirrors your walk with God, if you don't exercise gratitude in prayer and mean it, then you are controlled by self or "I." You live in a world where everything revolves around you. When ego controls your life, you are not concerned with the influence of others who brought you to church or nurtured your early faith or prayed for your salvation. Ego-driven people are concerned with what they have done to make them what they are. They want to magnify themselves beyond who they are.

But the believer who can get answers to prayer can influence others to realize the role of their spiritual growth. The four key words in Galatians 2:20 is the essence of Christianity, "Not I, but Christ." Christ fills a person who has learned when "Christ died, I died." In their co-crucifixion experience, they learn "Christ lives in me, and the life I now live, I live by the faith of the Son of God who loves me and gave Himself for me" (Galatians 2:20).

First, it is not you, but Christ who lives in you that gives you victory in your Christian life. Second, your life in the flesh will be a failure without Christ. Third, the faith of Christ will give you power to live and minister for Him. Fourth, it is not you or your ability or your power. No! Your new life is not a condition, it is a person, it is Jesus Christ when you embrace Galatians 2:20, you will be grateful for all Christ has done in you, and for you. Having a grateful attitude in prayer is the indispensable influence for answers to prayer.

Gratitude will also a mirror your appreciation for the influence of your family—father and mother in your life. Then you must include the influence of teachers, work associates, friends, and mentors. Those who help you at work have influenced you, as well as those you work with, and those who work for you. Gratitude recognizes them for their influence in your life.

Who was it that said, "no man is an island"? This famous saying reflected the influence that many have had in our life, both secular and especially spiritual. Think of those who taught you Christian values and godly habits—be thankful for them. Think of those who taught you Scriptures and doctrine—thank God for them. Think of those who have preached to you the example of Christian living, or they motivated you to surrender to Jesus Christ or follow Him. Be thankful for them.

There are no self-made Christians, and those who claim to be are probably like a _____. No, many have influenced your life, so be grateful to them.

WRAP UP GRATITUDE

There are six foundations to *gratitude-praying*. These six foundations mirror the previous chapter in the book. First, be grateful your sins are forgiven. You did nothing to be forgiven or cleansed of sin. Christ did it all. So, be grateful for "the blood of Jesus Christ that cleanses us from all sin" (1 John 1:7).

Second, be grateful for the opportunity to worship and praise the Lord, and for what that experience does for you. Remember the "Father seeks worship" (John 4:23). Don't glory in the skills of your worship, or the amount of time you worship, or the things you do in worship. Worship is all about Him, not about you. So, when you approach the Lord in praise/worship, be grateful for the opportunity to worship, the freedom to worship, and the immense privilege of worship.

The third indispensable word of effective praying is faith. Remember Jesus told His disciples on several occasions they had "weak faith." Is that a description of you? Don't glory in your faith and brag about the strength of our faith. Rather, let's be grateful in salvation. Let's be grateful that Jesus gives us His faith, this is called "indwelling faith." Paul said it best, "I live by the faith of the Son of God" (Galatians 2:20). Remember, your faith is not about what you do in worship, it is all about the One your worship.

The fourth indispensable is yielding. When we surrender ourselves, we do it to get the strength of Christ. When we yield ourselves and our ministry to God; we let God do His work in us and through us. When He answers, we are grateful.

The fifth indispensable is asking to get our prayers answered. When you ask a person for anything, you must be grateful when you receive it. Those who are not thankful are selfish...ignorant...blind...egotistical. When the Father answers any of your request, be thankful to Him...show gratitude.

The last indispensable is continual asking. God doesn't answer on the clock. It is not how long you prayed, nor how many times you prayed, or even if you break the record for time spent praying. The word *continue praying* points back to a relationship with God. Gratitude is continuing in that relationship. We continue because we love Him, because we enjoy fellowshipping with Him, and we know there is life and fullness of joy in His presence. We continue praying because we are grateful for all He has done, and we by faith know all He will do.

AFTERWORD

THIS book is about asking and answers—how God answers prayers. Whereas most books on prayer focus on the one praying, this book has analyzed both *how you pray* and *how God answers*. When you understand the answers to these two questions, you will be better able to pray.

Have you ever noticed how you give an everyday answer differently according to the person who calls you? You answer with *surprise* when someone calls your name in a crowd. You answer with *irritation* to a telephone call from an unwanted solicitor. You answer *impersonally* to a business e-mail. You *debate* when the other is wrong. You *defend* when attacked. So, don't be surprised when God answers differently to all the various ways you pray.

When you understand how God answers prayers, you will have more success in your intercession because you will know how to properly ask God for the things you pray.

Most books look at prayer from the front end—before you pray. This book looked at both before you pray and how God answers after you pray. How does God answer? When does God answer? Or, why we don't get what we request.

Did you know the word *answers* is not often found in the Bible? It's not mentioned nearly as often as the word *pray*. Many have written books on prayer but not many have written on answers. Why is that? Maybe we're self-motivated and think of ourselves when we pray. But shouldn't our prayer also be focused on God, the One to whom we pray?

This book was written on the premise that God answers prayer when we meet the conditions found in the *7 Indispensable Words For Effective Prayer*. One of the first occurrences of the word *answer* in Scripture is a reference to Jacob who built an altar unto God, saying, *"I will make an altar there to God, who answered me in the day of my distress and has been with me in the way which I have gone"* (Gen. 35:3). How did Jacob get an answer from God? He originally asked for God to *"be with me, and keep me in this way that I am going, and give me bread to eat and clothing to put on, so that I come back to my father's house in peace"* (Gen. 28:20-21).

Because God answered Jacob's prayer, he built an altar and sacrificed to God. (Jacob practiced the 7th indispensable condition, i.e., gratitude).

On many occasions throughout the sufferings of Job, he asks God to explain why he was in pain or why so many bad things happened to him. Finally, *"the Lord answered Job out of the whirlwind"* (Job 38:1; 40:1). If God answered Job, then He can answer you.

Moses, Aaron, Samuel, and the priest, *"They called upon the Lord, and He answered them"* (Ps. 99:6). God hears those who ask for answers.

Then Elijah confronted the false priests of Balaam, with the challenge, *"The God who answers by fire, He is God"* (1 Kings 18:24). So, God's people—like Elijah—expected answers to their intercessory prayers. That's why the Psalmist begged, *"You will answer us, O God"* (Ps. 65:5).

One of God's greatest invitations in the Bible is *"Call to Me, and I will answer you"* (Jer. 33:3). God in Heaven challenges you to "call on Him." He has promised, "I will answer."

You have the assurance that God knows your need before you ask (see Matt 6:8), and that He has put answers in motion, *"Before they call, I will answer"* (Isa. 65:24).

PART TWO

50 DAILY DEVOTIONS
7 Indispensable Words for Effective Prayer

Day 1

SIN BLOCKS PRAYER

"We know that God doesn't listen to sinners,
but He is ready to hear those who worship Him and do His will."

John 9:31, NLT

DID you see the word *indispensable* in the title to this series? One of the necessary words is forgiveness. God not only can answer your prayer when you sin, He won't ever listen. Is your prayer a one-way conversation, you doing all the talking and listening? Then your indispensable word is forgiveness. You must begin looking within to heal your broken relationship with God before you look up to Him for answers.

> *Lord, forgive me for all the times my sin has blocked my access to You. I confess my sin blinds*
> *me, so I cannot ever see what I have done wrong. I confess I am frustrated...open the eyes of*
> *my heart to see my sin, and to see what I must do. Amen.*

First, you must confess you have been blinded by your pride and prejudice. You must be willing to see your problems. You must admit your sin and confess it. Then take initiative to do something about your sin. Deal with your sin before answers will come.

> *Lord, forgive my sin. I want to be forgiven and clean (1 John 1:9). Restore my fellowship*
> *with You and let me talk with You. More than my request, I need to feel Your presence, and*
> *enjoy intimacy with You. Amen.*

READING:

John 9:24-33; 1 John 1:7-10

REFLECTION

Day 2

ARE MY HANDS CLEAN?

"Who may ascend into the hill of the Lord? Or who may stand in His holy place?
He who has clean hands and a pure heart."

Psalm 24:3-4

THE revival that swept the New Hebrides in the 19th century began when a group of laymen gathered in a barn to pray. One man continually held up his hands asking God, "Are my hands clean?" This led the group to confess their sins and pray for natural revival. The Lord used Duncan Campbell as preacher to call for people in all the towns and rural areas to get saved. The indispensable word for answers is *forgiveness*. It begins when you take responsibly for your condition before God as you search your heart and ask:

Lord, are my hands clean? I want Your blessing in my life and need answers to my requests.
Show me any hidden sin or any sin I have forgotten. I will continue to seek forgiveness.
Amen.

When you ask God to show the sin in your life, be certain that any sin God shows...can be cleansed by the blood of Christ. The old hymn asks, "What can wash away my sin?" God's answer, "Nothing but the blood of Jesus" (1 John 1:7, 9).

Lord, I confess my hands are not clean. Forgive my sin and cleanse me by the blood of
Christ. I will search my heat till I know I can come in prayer to You. Amen.

READING:

Psalm 24:1-10

REFLECTION

Day 3

WHAT CAN CLEANSE YOUR HEART?

"The blood of Jesus His son, cleanses us from all sin."

1 John 1:7

REMEMBER in yesterday devotional, the question was asked, "What can wash away my sin?" The answer, "Nothing but the blood of Jesus." The thing most precious to the Father is His Son Jesus. The thing most precious to Jesus is His life. What is necessary for life...blood. When you say Jesus gave His life, you include Jesus shedding His blood for you, when He died for you. It was Jesus' perfect substitute for your sin, Jesus died for your sin. It was Jesus' pardon for your sin penalty.

Lord, I asked You to cleanse me when I was saved. Thank You for cleansing me and giving me a new standing before the Father. Thank You for giving me prayer access to the Father. Amen.

The blood of Jesus restored your relationship to the Father, so you are now His child. But when daily life trips you up with secret sins or ignorant sins, or you break God's commandments presumptuously, you need your fellowship restored. You don't get saved again. No! You confess your sins and He restores you to His fellowship.

Lord, I confess I have ignorantly sinned, but also, I am weak, and I have shipped, but didn't mean to sin. Forgive me...cleanse me...restore me...please answer my prayers. Amen.

READING:

Psalm 51:1-19

REFLECTION

Day 4

IGNORANT SINS

"How can I know all the sins lurking in my heart? Cleanse me from these hidden faults. Keep your servant from deliberate sins! Don't let them control me. Then I will be free of guilt and innocent of great sin."

Psalm 19:12-13, NLT

THE old saying, "to get completely clean, you must completely confess." Could it be that when you pray for a request, there is a sin holding you back—a forgotten sin? Today's verse calls it a "hidden fault." It is hidden from most people and hidden from you. But it is not hidden from God. It could be an ignorant sin, you took something, but you didn't think it was wrong. Do you need to be forgiven of ignorant sins? No matter what the motivation or original intent, go the extra mile and confess any and all sin.

Lord, You have promised to forgive me and cleanse me from all iniquity when I confess my sins. I confess all I am a sinner, whether I remember it or not. I confess silently in my heart, and I will confess to another when need be (Matthew 5:23-24). Thank You for faithfully hearing me and forgiving me (1 John 1:9). Amen.

There is another area you must deal with that demands we must be perfect (Matthew 5:48). When we don't measure up to God's perfect standards—then confess your lack of perfection. God will give you the righteousness of Jesus Christ (2 Corinthians 5:21). When we come through the blood of Christ, we are as righteous as Jesus Christ.

Lord, I do not stand in my _____, nor my righteousness. I was born in sin and I have sinned. Forgive me...cleanse me...give me Christ righteousness...accept me...hear my prayers. Amen.

READING:

Matthew 5:13-26

REFLECTION

Day 5

CONFESSION

"He who covers his sins will not prosper,
But whoever confesses and forsakes them will have mercy."

Proverbs 28:13, NKJV

"Finally, I confessed all my sins to you and stopped trying to hide my guilt.
I said to myself, 'I will confess my rebellion to the Lord.'
And you forgave me! All my guilt is gone."

Psalm 32:5, NLT

WHAT is confession? It is more than admitting you have done wrong. It is more than agreeing with another's opinion of the crime/sin. First, Webster's meaning, "To acknowledge a fault, crime, or debt." Yes, it begins with acknowledgment, but the second is acknowledge your intent or to own up to your responsibility. Too often people only half-way confess. They say, "The man made me do it."(Eve). Or they excuse themselves, "I didn't know it was wrong." Or they might blame someone else, "Johnny made me do it." But biblical confession is acknowledging it was wrong and taking ownership of the sin.

Lord, I know I was wrong. I take responsibility, I sinned against you. Forgive me...I repent...I will serve You.. Amen.

Confession means you agree with God, it means you agree that your sin is as bad as God sees it. Then you go a step further, confessing means you "turn from the sin" and commit yourself to never going there again, or doing it again. When you forsake (repent), God will forget and accept you.

Lord, forgive me for shallow confessions in the past, and forgive me for trying to wiggle out of responsibility. I confess I sinned...forgive me...cleanse me...accept me...I completely repent and give it up. Now I need your strength to live for You. Amen.

READING:

John 21:12-25

REFLECTION

Day 6

CONFESSION FOR FORGIVENESS AND CLEANSING

"But if we confess our sins to him, he is faithful and just to forgive us our sins and to cleanse us from all wickedness."

1 John 1:9, NLT

THERE are two things that you want from God when you confess your sin(s) to Him. Some have confessed and still felt guilty, so maybe they keep confessing and confessing. They have confessionitis, i.e., they feel guilty. Don't be that way. Confess to God and "he that cometh to God must believe that He is..." (Hebrews 11:6). If you have faith to confess all sin, then claim by faith to accept His response. What is His first promise? "The Lord is faithful." That means God will be faithful to do for you what He has promised! He promises to forgive, and He will do it.

Lord, I confess my sins(s) to You because You invited me to do it. Thank You for Your faithfulness to forgive me, as You promised. I accept forgiveness. And thank You for being "just" I stand in Your acceptance. Amen.

The first thing in today's verse is God's faithfulness to forgive your sins. The second thing is God will forgive and cleanse us from all wickedness. That means God will clean your record. He will wipe your record in Heaven clean. Now you must act in faith and based on your new standing with God, you can pray effectively.

Lord, I come into Your presence and I stand in the forgiveness of Jesus Christ. Now I want Your fellowship and I want You to manifest Yourself to me. Then, I will present my prayer requests. Amen.

READING:

Acts 5:23-35

REFLECTION

_____

_____

_____

_____

_____

_____

_____

_____

_____

_____

Day 7

CONFESS COMPLETELY

"I prayed to the Lord my God and confessed: 'O Lord, you are a great and awesome God! You always fulfill your covenant and keep your promises of unfailing love to those who love you and obey your commands. But we have sinned and done wrong. We have rebelled against you and scorned your commands and regulations.'"

Daniel 9:4-5, NLT

WHAT kind of confession of sin does God want from you? Not so you will be cleaner than you have ever been. No! that is comparing your present cleanliness with previous times you were able to pray. But that is not good enough, you must confess, "All our righteousness are like filthy rags" (Isaiah 64:6, NKJV). A complete confession leads to complete cleanliness. "Come now, and let us reason together, says the Lord, 'Though your sins are like scarlet, they shall be as white as snow; though they are red like crimson, they shall be as wool'" (Isaiah 1:18, NKJV). The old farmer said, "If you have messed up, you should fess up!"

Lord, look into my heart, I confess all my sins, forgive me. But go deeper Lord, examine the intents of my heart to see my faults, and look at all my weak excuses and half-hearted efforts and forgive my failings. I need cleansing. Amen.

Why must you confess all your sins, because God already knows your sins. Remember, He is your omniscient God—He knows all things, actual and possible. He is omnipresent God; He is always present at every place all the time. So, He fully knows your weakness, more than you realize. Your full confession puts you on His level of examining your motives. He knows...He will forgive...He will restore...He will use you.

Lord, give me the honesty to confess all my sins. Give me strength when I see all my sins to continue praying. Hear my complete confession and forgive me. I want to serve You. Please answer my prayers. Amen.

READING:

Daniel 9:3-19

REFLECTION

Day 8

BEGIN WITH PRAISE AND WORSHIP

"Worship the Lord with gladness, come before Him singing with joy...enter His gates with thanksgiving, go into His courts with praise."

Psalm 100:2-3, NLT

BEGIN your praying to the Lord with praise, thanksgiving, and worship. Why? Because the Psalmist instructed us this is an *entrance* Psalm into God's temple. Pray the Book of Psalms. It is the primary book in the Bible on praise and worship. So, we ought to follow its example. Begin worshiping the moment you enter His presence. If you enter the room of the U.S. President, or the British Prime Minister, or the King of Denmark, you immediately become aware of the Sovereign's presence. You would focus all your attention on him. The same is with God. You cannot enter God's presence without realizing His presence. So, prepare your heart and mind to meet God in prayer. What would you say first?

> *Lord, Your almighty power created the earth, planets, and trillions of burning stars. I praise You for creating humans in Your image, I thank you for giving me life and a challenge to live for You. May I serve You and worship You. Amen.*

The depth of your worship of God is a sincere acknowledgment of His worth and value. "Praise Him according to His excellent greatness!" (Psalm 150:2). You must praise and worship Him because of who He is? "Worthy is the Lamb" (Revelation 5:12). Then worship Him for all He has done for you.

Lord, I am nothing, You are everything. I am empty, You are full of mercy...love...and grace. I bow to ask forgiveness and then I thank You for forgiveness and cleansing me (1 John 1:9). Thank You for everything! Amen.

READING:

Psalm 146:1-21

REFLECTION

WORSHIP IN PRAYER

"Pray like this, 'Our Father in heaven, may Your name be kept holy.'"

Matthew 6:9, NLT

BEGIN your prayer with praise or worship because Jesus taught in the Lord's Prayer to begin recognizing the Father's holiness. This is worship in prayer. The King James says, "Hallowed be Thy name," which means to honor God's name, or to reverence God's name. Since the angels cry, "holy, holy, holy" to God on His throne, how else can we come into His presence, except to follow their example and cry "holy is His name." When you ask the nature of God, many say He is spirit, or He is love, or He is good. But many think God's holiness is the essence that influences all life on earth.

> *Lord, I come into Your presence repeating, "holy...holy...holy," because that is what You are. I worship You for Your love and mercy that holds back Your judgment of sin...on me. I thank You for Your love, but I bow and worship Your holiness. Amen.*

There are many reasons to worship God...because of His majesty (Psalm 69:34)...because of creation (Psalm 145:10)...because of His guidance in life (Psalm 71:9)...and because He has saved you and given you a new life (Acts 3:8).

> *Lord, for all these reasons I praise You for everything You have done for others and for me. But I move from praise to worship as I bow to give all worship to You for everything You have done for me. Amen.*

READING:

Psalm 150

REFLECTION

_____

_____

_____

_____

_____

_____

_____

_____

_____

_____

_____

Day 10

WORSHIP THE FATHER

"But the hour is coming—in fact it is here already—when true
worshipers will worship the Father in spirit and truth!
That is the kind of worship the Father wants."

John 4:23, Jerusalem Bible

W HY must you begin your prayers with praise and worship? Because that is what the Father wants. Jesus told us that truth, because He wants you to approach the Father with worship, so you would enjoy His fellowship and get your request answered. Yes, worship is important to get your prayers answered, but you want more than answers. Because prayer is the relationship you want Him...you want to enjoy Him...you want to listen to Him...you want to carry His presence from your prayer time into your everyday life. When you learn what the Father wants, and you give worship to Him, then you get what you ask for in prayers.

Lord, I come obediently because You invited me. I come worshiping because You seek wor-
ship. I come asking because Jesus told me to ask (John 13:14). I come just to enjoy Your
presence, because You will answer. Amen.

Did you see the phrase in today's verse, "the kind of worship the Father wants"? Forget about what you want to ask Him. Before you ask for what you want, think about what God wants. After all, He is the One giving and you are the one receiving. Give the Father the worship He wants from you. If you don't know what worship is, or how to give it...just as Him, that will begin your worship.

Father, I want to worship You with the type of praise and adoration that You want. Show
me in Scriptures and speak to my heart, I will learn and follow...I will worship. Amen.

READING:

Psalm 147:1-20

REFLECTION

Day 11

TOTAL PRAISE AND WORSHIP

"Let God's people shout loud His glory, let them sing loudly His greatness.
Let His highest praise fill their hearts and lives."

Psalm 149:5-6, ELT

YOU must begin your prayer with praise and worship because it is the first response of His people who worship Him. It is their loudest and most thunderous response to His glory and power. Worship Him because you are in His presence, what else can you do but express your love...and gratitude...and yieldedness...and your worship. Just as you cannot stand in fire without being burnt, and you can be immersed in ice water without freezing, so you cannot enter the presence of your God without expressing a total response of all your gratitude and worship.

Lord, I come into Your presence again asking for the cleansing blood of Christ to prepare me for You presence. I enter Your throne, knowing You created the world, Your laws control everything and I am needy. I come humbly to worship Your majesty before I ask for my requests. Amen.

Today's verse describes your response in God's presence. You must shout loud, giving Him glory. Is there any other response? You must "sing loudly His praise." Do you remember any congregational singing where you sang praises to God at the top of your voice? You must "let His highest praise fill your heart and life." What is the greatest praise or compliment you have ever given to God? Do it now!

Lord, I am only human, but I want to give you all my love. And I am not talented, but I want to serve You the best I am able. And I am not a great singer, but I want to sing to You the highest praise that any human has ever given.. Amen.

READING:

Psalm 149:1-9

REFLECTION

Day 12

SACRIFICE OF WORSHIP

*"Therefore, by Him let us continually offer the sacrifice of praise to God,
that is, the fruit of our lips, giving thanks to His name."*

Hebrews 13:15, NKJV

*"David said, I will not present burnt offerings to
the Lord my God that have cost me nothing"*

2 Samuel 24:24, NLT

YOU must begin your prayer with the sacrifice of worship or praise. Have you thought what is involved in a sacrifice? First, there is a loss incurred to you the giver. Second, you give that which is valuable or desirable. Third, you give because there is a higher or more authoritative claim. Those three definitions of sacrifice in reverse describes what happens when you worship. First you give up your time, and your claim on your life to God. Second, you give your time to God, your energy to God, and your treasures to God. Finally, you give all worship to God because He is a higher authority than anyone in the world. He has the highest claim on your life.

Lord, I offer You the sacrifice of time, I give You complete attention, sacrificing anything else. I give you my talent and all my creative ability, making You first in my life. Finally, I give you all my treasures, i.e., money and possessions to use for Your glory and ministry. Amen.

A young married couple sacrifices for their children because they love them. They do the same for each other because of love. That is the reason you sacrifice to God because He loves you...because He is worth the sacrifice...because He first gave Himself to you...because He will give more back to you than you can ever give to Him.

> *Lord, I am only human, but I want to give you all my love. And I am not talented, but I want to serve You the best I am able. And I am not a great leader, but I want to give You the highest praise that any human has ever given You. Amen.*

READING:

Psalm 149:1-9

REFLECTION

Day 13

BOASTING

"I will boast only in the Lord."

Psalm 34:2, NLT

"In God we boast all day long, and praise Your name forever"

Psalm 44:8, NKJV

YOU begin your prayer with praise and worship because God alone deserves it. You don't brag on yourself, nor do you enlarge your ego. No! Our boasting is in God because He has done so much for us. While boasting is a word used in the world to build up one's self, or when we claim recognition, we think we deserve. But the Psalmists boasted in God. Why? Because they knew in themselves was not any good thing in God's holy sight. They knew their weakness and failings, and they even knew their sins. But they know God was holy...God was meaningful...God was powerful...God was their protector...and they know God was their salvation after death.

Lord, I boast in Your salvation, thank You for forgiveness of sin. I boast in Your mercy, thank You for eternal life with You in Heaven. I boast of my changed life. Jesus is living in my heart and I serve Him. Amen.

When you bring your request to God, it is not about your goodness, nor about your ability to pray, nor about your faithfulness in service to God. It is about God...His glory...His power...His ability to answer your prayers. Come looking only to God.

Lord, I come with bowed head, I don't look at others, and I don't look around. I look only to You. If I have any boasting it is in Your goodness and grace. I love You and worship You. Amen.

READING:

Psalm 148:1-14

REFLECTION

_____

_____

_____

_____

_____

_____

_____

_____

_____

Day 14

LIFTING HANDS

"Then Ezra praised the Lord, the great God, and all the people chanted,
'Amen! Amen!' as they lifted their hands. Then they bowed down
and worshiped the Lord with their faces to the ground."

Nehemiah 8:6, NLT

YOU begin your prayers with praise and worship because of the many examples of God's people in Scriptures. Nehemiah, the cupbearer for King Xerus in Persia was used of God to rebuild the walls of Jerusalem. When he finished, Ezra the scribe led the people in dedicating the walls and the people to the Lord. Did you see how Ezra began; he praised the Lord with their faces to the ground. This is an extreme example when we give God our best. They began with praise and worship. Both leaders and people. That means when we come to the Lord, we should first praise Him for all He has done. Then we should worship Him for who He is.

Lord, like the refugees returning to Jerusalem, I begin with praise and worship. You died for
our sins, You have forgiven our sins, and You have filled us with Your power. We praise You
for what You did for us and we worship You for who You are. Amen.

Just as the followers of God in Scriptures approached God with praise and worship, so we should approach Him the same way. Our prayers are often so *earthy,* but our prayers should be *Heavenly,* we should look for God's glory in all we ask and do.

Lord, I come with my request, and they seem so small when compared to Your glory. I wor-
ship You for Your glory, please answer the prayers I make to You. Amen.

READING:

Psalm 145:1-21

REFLECTION

Day 15

FAITH

"For by grace are you saved through faith."

Ephesians 2:8

THE key to getting your prayers answer is *faith*. When God sees your faith, He mobilizes your answer. Amen! But, look carefully at faith. First, it is a response to the Word of God. On several occasions in Scriptures the Bible is called *faith* (Jude 3; 1 Timothy 5:8), the Bible is the content of faith. Next, you must be saved by *faith*, you believe that Jesus died for your sins and His blood cleanses you from all sin (Ephesians 1:7). From the human view, this is called *conversion*. It is when you repent from the old life of sin, and you are converted to the new life in Jesus Christ. From a Heavenly view this is called regeneration, you are born again (John 3:5-7) and given a new nature to live for God (2 Corinthians 5:17).

Father, my saving-faith has given me a new relationship to You. Now I come to You through praying-faith because I am Your child. Teach me the joys and rewards of praying in faith. Amen.

Saving-faith gives you a new relationship with your Heavenly Father. Now you can come to Him, just like a child asks for those from their earthly father. You can ask your Heavenly Father to teach you...lead you...protect you...and use you in ministry. The creditability of your *praying-faith* is built on the assurance of your *saving-faith*.

Father, I come to You because You are my Heavenly Father. I need to learn many things, teach me. I need direction, guide me. I need to make decision, give me wisdom. I have doubts, hold me close, and give me the assurance of eternal life. Amen.

READING:

Ephesians 2:1-22

REFLECTION

Day 16

BIBLE PRAYING

"Contend earnestly for the faith which was
once for all delivered to the saints."

Jude 3

THERE are many ways to pray in faith, but the one that is most foundational required of all valid prayer, is praying in the faith of the Word of God. What is this? It is another way to describe *Bible-praying* or making intercession according to Scriptures. There are three ways to pray according to the Bible (1) its authority, (2) its life, and (3) its Jesus Himself. So, first when you pray in faith you are interceding according to the principles found in Scriptures. Didn't Jesus tell us, "Abide in Me and My words...ask" (Romans 15:7). When you pray according to the Word/Scriptures, Jesus will answer. Then the Bible has life. John called it, The Word of life (1 John 1:1). You believe the Word for eternal life, and you pray the words from God to give life and answers to your prayers.

> *Father, the Bible is my foundation and my salvation is based on the Bible. But more than*
> *that, the Bible is life, and I love the hymn, "Sing them over again to me, wonderful words*
> *of life." I come praying through the life I have in Scriptures. Amen.*

But when you pray based on the Bible, you are asking Jesus, because the Bible said, "In the beginning was the Word...and the Word was God" (John 1:1). Jesus is God incarnate in the flesh, and Jesus is God inspired in Scriptures. So, when you pray the Scriptures, you are praying based on Jesus, you are praying filled with Jesus, praying motivated by Jesus, praying with Jesus.

> *Father, I come praying to You, as I pray with Jesus. He is my Savior and my Lord. He said*
> *to ask in His name and You would answer. So, I come asking in Jesus' name. Amen.*

READING:

John 1:1, 14-18; 6:60-71

REFLECTION

Day 17

JUSTIFIED BY FAITH

"Therefore, having been justified by faith, we have peace with God through our Lord Jesus Christ, through whom also we have access by faith into this grace in which we stand, and rejoice in hope of the glory of God."

Romans 5:1-2, NKJV

"My Father has placed your sins on Me, the sinless One, and My Father put My righteousness on you. Now you stand perfect before My Father."

2 Corinthians 5:21, BBJ

WHEN you begin to pray in faith, remember there are several expressions of faith in Scriptures, i.e., saving faith, doctrinal faith, etc. Today let's look at your new position of being justified by faith in Christ. This is not what you experience, like living by faith. No, this is nonexperiential, it is your new position in Christ as you stand in Christ before the Father. Because Christ has perfect righteousness, you stand there in Christ's righteousness. That means in God's sight, you have never sinned—just as Jesus never sinned. Because you stand perfect in Heaven, now pray by faith on earth.

Father, I come to You through the perfection of Jesus. Forgive my sin, look on me as You would look on Your Son Jesus. Now Father, I pray to You in faith to answer the request I present. Amen.

The secret of living for Jesus is to claim His presence in your life for power to live victoriously on this earth according to your position in Christ in Heaven. And the secret of victorious prayer is to pray in faith on earth based on your standing in Jesus before the Father. Your human life is not the bases of your prayer, but it is the faith of Jesus in you.

Father, I come expectantly into Your presence because I come with Your Son, Jesus Christ. I make my prayers not based on my human ability or my Christian walk. I pray in the power of Jesus' perfection. I come praying in Jesus' name. Amen.

READING:

Romans 5:1-11; 2 Corinthians 5:17-21

REFLECTION

Day 18

INDWELLING FAITH

"I live by the faith of the Son of God, who loved me and gave Himself for me."

Galatians 2:20

*"I answered, 'Let God's faith control you. Verify, if you will say to a mountain,
be removed and thrown into the sea and you don't doubt but believe
that you will receive what you ask, you shall have it.'"*

Mark 11:22-24, BBJ

THERE are several expressions of faith such as saving faith, doctrinal faith, and living (daily) by faith. But learn to pray with indwelling faith. That is when Jesus lives in your heart and you release Him to pray through you for requests. Jesus' faith is powerful—stronger than yours—and Jesus faith is effective—while you have doubts. Therefore, when you pray with Jesus—and He prays through you—God will honor your request. The indwelling Jesus and His faith is one of your most powerful tools in prayer.

Father, I come to You with Jesus praying in His authority and praying in His mighty power. Let His powerful faith give strength to my weak faith so You can answer the request I make today. Amen.

You have weak faith as did Abraham (Romans 4:19). But God worked in Abraham's life so that He was, "strengthened in faith" (Romans 4:20). Because of Abraham's faith he became the father of faith, and the father of Israel. This illustration holds out the promise to you that your faith can be strengthened and you can pray victoriously in faith.

Father, I come praying through Jesus' faith. I confess that my faith is weak like Abraham's.
Give me strength and faith to believe in Jesus' miraculous prayer-answering power. Amen.

READING:

Mark 11:2-26; Romans 4:11-25

REFLECTION

Day 19

WALK DAILY BY FAITH

"We walk by faith, not by sight."

2 Corinthians 5:7

THE key to effective prayer is to make sure you are daily walking by faith. This is not being saved by faith, that begins your faith walk with Christ. This is not being justified by faith, that is your new position in Christ when God declares you have the righteousness of Christ (Romans 5:1). You need both saving faith and justifying faith to walk daily in faith. But walking by faith means obeying the Scriptures, i.e., "walking in the light" (2 John 6) and "walk in truth" (2 John 4). Your challenge is to have Abraham's faith, "Abraham obeyed..." (Hebrews 11:8). To walk by faith is to live according to Scriptures.

Lord, I prayed by faith, but the answer did not come. I will go back to check the require-ments of Scripture. Now I will pray according to the direction of Scriptures and I will pray following the principles of Scriptures. Amen.

Look at Hebrews 11 to see those who lived and prayed by faith. "By faith Abel offered...sacrifice" (v. 4). "By faith Noah...prepared an ark" (v. 5). By faith Moses choosing...the people of God" (v. 24-25). Other examples of Faith—Gideon, Samuel, and David. We know their victories, but also their "trials...scourging...chains...imprisonment" (v. 36). Their faith was effective because they obeyed God.

Lord, walking by faith is wonderful because I walk with You. I believe in You, so I will pray in faith. Even then I know there will be difficulties, trials, and hardships. But you are worthy. Amen.

READING:

Hebrews 11:1-40

REFLECTION

Day 20

MUSTARD SEED FAITH

"Afterward the disciples asked Jesus privately, 'Why couldn't we cast out that demon?' 'You don't have enough faith,' Jesus told them. 'I tell you the truth, if you had faith even as small as a mustard seed, you could say to this mountain, 'Move from here to there,' and it would move. Nothing would be impossible.'"

Matthew 17:19-20, NLT

AS you continue praying in faith, your *mustard seed faith* will continue to grow. When the disciples could not cast a demon out of a boy, they asked, why? Jesus answered, "You don't have enough faith." He said if your faith is as big as a mustard seed, then you could do it. A mustard seed is among the smallest seeds and the full-grown mustard plant is among the largest. That means faith can grow. First you must want faith to grow and pray, "increase our faith." Second, you must abide in fellowship with Jesus (John 15:7) for it is His power that answers, not the size of your faith. Third, you must apply your faith in ministry. "We receive...whatever we ask...because we obey" (1 John 3:22, NLT).

Lord, my faith is small, but I worship You with all my heart and I love to serve You in ministry. Please grow my faith to believe in great answers to prayer. Amen.

Jerry Falwell, pastor of Thomas Road Baptist Church and founder of Liberty University, which is the largest evangelical faith college in the world, was asked to talk about his great faith. He answered, "I don't have great faith...." The report started to turn away when Falwell said, "Let me tell you about my great God!" The source of mighty faith is not in you or anyone else. When you have full confidence in a mighty God, you have mighty faith. What is the answer? Get more of God and let Him control your life.

Jesus, I come struggling and empty. I admit I am weak, and I need Your mighty power. Work through me. I need Your indwelling transformation. Jesus live in my life and give me mighty faith. Amen.

READING:

Mark 9:14-29

REFLECTION

Day 21

ASSURANCE FAITH

"Keep on asking, and you will receive what you ask for. Keep on seeking, and you will find. Keep on knocking, and the door will be opened to you. For everyone who asks, receives. Everyone who seeks, finds. And to everyone who knocks, the door will be opened."

Matthew 7:7-8, NLT

"The apostles said to the Lord, "Show us how to increase our faith."

Luke 17:5, NLT

CONTINUE to ask God to grow your faith because your heart knows God will answer this prayer. Maybe the answer will come when you least expect it. Maybe not the way you want God to answer. What is the assurance that God will answer? It is found in today's verse. First "keep on asking" (v. 7), then the assurance "everyone who asks, receives" (v. 8). This promise of God to answer is reliable. Therefore, don't let your faith waver in God's ability to answer. Isn't faith "looking to God first...looking to God continually...looking to God eternally.

Lord, I pray with the disciples, "increase our faith" (Luke 17:5). I want more faith to get answers for my prayers. I want more faith to make me a stronger Christian. I want more faith to glory You. Amen.

Because you don't know why the answer hasn't come, keep on praying. Because you don't know the future and what you will need, keep on praying. Because God put a burden in your heart for the answer, keep on praying. The only one who knows the future is God, so keep on praying. Because prayer is a relationship with God, keep that relationship warm, keep on praying in faith.

Lord, You are the only One I trust, and You are the reason I keep praying for my requests. I look to You and not to circumstances and not to the calendar. Lord I look to You. Amen.

READING:

Luke 2:25-38

REFLECTION

_____

_____

_____

_____

_____

_____

_____

_____

_____

_____

Day 22

PARTNERSHIP WITH GOD

"We are partners with Christ when we are steadfast in prayer."

Hebrews 3:14, ELT

"We are fellow workers with God."

1 Corinthians 3:9, Jerusalem Bible

PRAY is partnership with God. It is the high privilege of entering God's presence to talk with Him about your needs and plans for the day. You are a worker for God, and you are called to serve Him. All that you want to do must be approved by Him. Therefore, one of the first things to do in prayer is yield to God. Some pray, "I surrender" others pray, "Thy will be done." Still others pray, "I yield to you."

Lord, I pray with the disciples, "increase our faith" (Luke 17:5). I want more faith to get answers for my prayers. I want more faith to make me a stronger Christian. I want more faith to glory You. Amen.

Because you don't know why the answer hasn't come, keep on praying. Because you don't know the future and what you will need, keep on praying in faith. Because God put a burden in your heart for the answer, keep on praying in faith. The only one who knows the future is God, so keep on praying in faith. Because prayer is a relationship with God, keep that relationship warm, keep on praying in faith.

Lord, You are the only One I trust, and You are the reason I keep praying for my requests. I look to You and not to circumstances and not to the calendar. Lord I look to You. Amen.

READING:

Luke 2:25-38

REFLECTION

Day 23

YIELDING IN PRAYER

[After the conversion of Saul/Paul] *"So he, trembling and astonished, said, 'Lord, what do You want me to do?'"*

Acts 9:6, NKJV

THE important things about prayer is finding God's will and then surrendering to God to do it. Once God's priority is settled in your mind, then you begin praying about how you are going to do God's will. It is important that you not hanging on to things that are for your selfish purpose, (James 4:2-3). Sometimes the request you make in prayers are good in themselves, but they may not be God's priority. So, the first step in effective praying is yielding to God to find what He wants you to do. "Not what I want, but what You want."

Father, I have asked for a lot of things in the past that didn't get answered. Other times You have answered. Help me know Your will so I pray for the right things and pray the right way. So, I begin this prayer, "Father I yield my will to You, help me ask for the things You want done." Amen.

Yielding in prayer is always the best way to begin your prayers. Many things may be good, but may not be what the Father wants you to have. Sometimes your requests are premature. Yield your schedule to God and wait for His answer. Sometimes, your request are going in the wrong direction, you are telling God how to answer your request. Yield to God. Let Him answer. Sometimes your request is contrary to what God is doing. Yield continue making your request.

Lord, I yield to Your time to answer. I yield to Your method of answers. I yield now You will answer. I even yield my desires for the answer, Your will be done. Amen.

READING:

James 4:1-17

REFLECTION

Day 24

YIELDED ATTITUDE

"Don't you realize that you can choose your own master? You can choose sin (with death) or else obedience (with acquittal). The one to whom you offer yourself—he will take you and be your master, and you will be his slave."

Romans 6:16, TLB

WHEN you come to pray, don't try to tell God what to do with your requests. You must bring a yielded attitude to God. Be willing to become what He wants. Be willing to do what He asks. Be willing to give to Him what He asks. And when you ask something from God, make sure it is what God wants done. Therefore, at the beginning of your prayer, surrender your will to God. Be willing to ask what He wants to give, and be willing to surrender yourself to do His will and you become His slave.

Father, I begin my prayer by yielding my complete life to You today. I surrender my body to do Your will. I surrender my time and talents to accomplish Your plans for me today. I surrender my prayers to You; may I ask what You want me to ask. Amen.

Yes, prayer is a relationship with God. You have plans for today, so does the Father. To make this day successful for eternity's sake; yield your plans to God's plans. Yield your desires to God's desires. Yield your prayers to God, asking Him to help you pray properly, and to ask for the right things.

Father, I ask You to open my spiritual eyes to see this day through Your eyes. Help me to ask and pray according to Your plans. I want to glorify You in all I do and pray, therefore, I yield everything to You. Amen.

READING:

Romans 6:12-22

REFLECTION

Day 25

GOD FIRST

"With eyes wide open to the mercies of God, I beg you, my brothers, as an act of intelligent worship, to give him your bodies, as a living sacrifice, consecrated to him and acceptable by him...let God remold your minds from within, so that you may prove in practice that the plan of God for you is good, meets all his demands and moves towards the goal of true maturity."

Romans 12:1-2, Philips

THE basic human desire is to possess things, time, and everything around you. But the Father wants you to look at life differently. He wants you to give up your selfishness, and make Him first in all you do, others second, and yourself last in priority. When you put God first, self doesn't lose; it wins. Remember Paul said, "For me to live is Christ" (Philippians 1:21).

Father help me reprioritize my desires. I want You first in my life. To do that, I surrender to You. Come sit on the throne of my life, and give me an eternal reason to live. Amen.

You begin effective praying when you begin by yielding your body and mind to the Lord. This act is called worship, and what is worship, it is giving the *worthship* to God that belongs to Him. Don't think of yielding to God as you are giving up; like one army surrendering to another. No! Your act of yielding to God is the doorway to worship. When you worship God, everything is focused on Him. Forget what you gave up, it is nothing compared to God's glory and God's blessing in your life. Prayer-yielding is the very best way to begin approaching God. Then you get Him on your side as you worship Him.

Father, I begin praying by yielding to You everything. I give You my possessions, I give You my body, I give You my mind...take everything and use them for Your glory. When I yield, I am not losing anything, I am getting Your presence in my life and a whole new reason to live. Amen.

READING:

Philippians 3:1-21

REFLECTION

Day 26

GOD'S WILL AND PLAN

"For whoever does the will of God is My brother and My sister and mother."

Mark 3:35, NKJV

"Do not be unwise, but understand what the will of the Lord is."

Ephesians 5:17, NKJV

GOD has a will for you or a plan for your life. God's original will was His original plan for Adam and Eve in the Garden of Eden. But sin messed that up. So, now God has a plan for us to live in a sin dominated world. He wants us to glorify Him in all we do in this world. So, when you approach God in prayer, how do you pray about His will for you, and His particular plan for your life? First, you should yield your will and plans to Him, and determine to live for God. Second, pray, "Thy will be done" (Matthew 6:9).

Father I humble myself before You, realizing I have done my will and accomplished my plan for my life. Forgive me. I yield my will to Your will. Give me wisdom to see Your plan for my life, and give me strength to do it. Amen.

The will of God is a noun, it is the plan that God has for your life. But the will of God is also a verb, He has an answer for every decision you face. God's active will can direct you to find His plan for your life. Whereas you may not be able to pray about every small decision, then surrender your life to God's will at the beginning of each day. And of course, seek Him and pray about those crucial decisions that determine the focus of your life.

Father, I come at the beginning of this day, yielding my decisions to Your will. May I always make decisions in keeping with Your plan for my life. Then, I surely will pray to seek Your will about the big decisions I will face. Amen.

READING:

Ephesians 5:1-21

REFLECTION

Day 27

PLANS FOR YOU

*"For I know the plans I have for you," says the Lord.
"They are plans for good and not for disaster,
to give you a future and a hope."*

Jeremiah 29:11, NLT

GOD has a plan for your life. There are four steps that are life-changing. First, the plan of your life is not your decision what you shall do or be, it is God's plan. Pray to understand it. Second, God already has a plan. Your task is to find it and do it. Third, your loving God wants you to live His plan because it is good for you, not a disaster. Fourth, God's plan has a beginning development in the middle, and a perfect ending for your life. When you fight His plan, you are resisting God's best for you. Some think their plans are better. We have seen enough people mess up their lives. So, accept God's plan that is good for you and not a disaster.

Father, once again I have come to the end of myself. I want a good life, so I yield myself to You. Lead me to Your good plan and show me Your perfect will for my life (Romans 12:1-2). Amen.

God has a plan specifically for you. However, you must yield to God and pray to know the right plan for your life. Beyond knowing, you must give effort to work His plan in your life. It may not come easy. Finally, constantly yield your selfish desires and plans to Him. Pray for guidance, ask for strength to do it, and finally trust God to protect you and help you accomplish His plan.

Father, I believe You have a specific plan for my life. I yield to You, and give up my plans for my life. Help me see Your plan, give me wisdom to follow it, and protect me from sin and satan as I attempt to do it. I need Your strength to accomplish Your plan in my life. Amen.

READING:

Jeremiah 29:1-14

REFLECTION

Day 28

NOT MY WILL

"He went a little farther and fell on His face, and prayed, saying,
O My Father, if it is possible, let this cup pass from Me; nevertheless,
not as I will, but as You will."'

Matthew 26:39, NKJV

EFFECTIVE prayers come by yielding yourself to God. Look at Jesus our example. In the Garden of Gethsemane Jesus asked His Father to take away the cup He had to drink the following day at Calvary. Jesus was going to take the sins of the world upon Himself and suffer the judgment of death for all sinners. He did not want to do it. Notice the first time Jesus resisted, but then yielded. "Not as I will, but as You will." Sometimes you will realize God is not going to answer your prayers, so you must yield to Him. "Not My will but Yours be done." But just as quickly Jesus asked a second time to remove the cup, but had to pray a second time, "Your will be done" (26:42). Have you ever struggled with the will of God?

Father, since prayer is a relationship to You, forgive me when I didn't understand Your "no."
Teach me to pray like Jesus, not my will, but thine be done." Amen.

To become the sin of the world was so great that Jesus came back a third time. "So, He (Jesus) left them, went away again, and prayed the third time, saying the same words" (26:44). Have you ever gone back to the Father three times about something you didn't want to do? We are not deity and don't understand the issue of becoming sin—all sin. But Jesus the third time prayed the same words, i.e., "Thy will be done."

Lord, forgive me when I have not been quick to obey You. I want Your best for my life, I want Your will in all things I do, and I want to become the person You want me to be. I surrender all. Amen.

READING:

Matthew 26:36-46

REFLECTION

Day 29

ASK!

"You can ask for anything in My name, and I will do it, so that the Son can bring glory to the Father. Yes, ask Me for anything in My name, and I will do it!"

John 14:13-14, NLT

TODAY you begin the fifth week in this series of *7 Indispensable Words for Effective Prayer*. The effective word is *Ask*! Don't begin asking for selfish requests, the way you usually ask for things on earth. Today's verse tells us to ask on Jesus' authority, i.e., "ask in My name." Human fathers have given their children what they ask, and that may be your approach to prayer. But now step up to the most important reason to ask in prayer. Ask in the authority of Jesus' name because He wants to be glorified in your life. And yes, He will give you what you ask because you are serving Him. Remember today's verse tells you to use Jesus' authority when praying.

Jesus, I come praying to You because You invited me to ask. But I realize the purpose of my prayer-authority is for Your glory, and for Your ministry, and because You indwell me. So, I come humbly saying, "thank You!" Amen.

Today's verse focuses on asking in Jesus' name so the Son can bring glory to the Father in Heaven. That is the reason your prayers will be heard and answered. So, be careful you are not asking for selfish reasons, or for schemes, or to protect your reputation (James 4:1-14). God knows your heart before you speak (Psalm 139:4).

Lord, I confess my sins and ask for cleansing. I want to pray for honest requests from an honest heart. I want You to hear my requests because I come in the authority of Jesus' name for the Father to glorify Jesus. Amen.

READING:

John 14:13-31

REFLECTION

Day 30

ABUNDANT JOY

"I tell you the truth, you will ask the Father directly, and He will grant your request because you use My name. You haven't done this before. Ask, using My name, and you will receive, and you will have abundant joy."

John 16:23-24, NLT

IN today's verse Jesus said, "ask the Father directly" (v. 23). Recognize that all prayers go to the Father sitting on the throne in Heaven. You pray directly to the Father but use Jesus' name because of the intimate relationship between the Father and Son. The Father will not turn down a request from His Son. So, use that relationship in prayer...you will be heard. But make sure you meet all the requirements—(see the devotions for the rest of this week). You can pray with confidence when you deliver your requests through your relationship with the Son to the Father.

Father, I come to You through Jesus with my request. I confess my sins, and I ask You to forgive my doubts and fears. Give me confidence to pray directly to You. Amen.

You could not get to see the President of the United States without going through security, or Washington officials, or some other source of authority. But you go directly to the Heavenly Father because you pray in Jesus' name. Using His name is your authority. Of course, either the Father or Son could answer your request. But this way there is no confusion. You meet the first qualification of *confession* of sin to establish a relationship with the Father. Second, worship. Third ask in faith. Now you have a prayer-relationship with the Father.

Father, I come in prayer-relationship to You. I come into Your presence with my request. I come in Jesus' name asking for the things upon my heart. Amen.

READING:

John 16:5-33

REFLECTION

Day 31

DOUBT?

"If you need wisdom, ask our generous God, and he will give it to you. He will not rebuke you for asking. But when you ask him, be sure that your faith is in God alone. Do not waver, for a person with divided loyalty is as unsettled as a wave of the sea that is blown and tossed by the wind. Such people should not expect to receive anything from the Lord."

James 1:5-7, NLT

NOTICE the demand of faith, "when you ask, you must believe and not doubt" (1:6, *NIV*). Doubting is the opposite of faith. *The King James* calls it "wavering." *The Phillips Bible* says, "without secret doubt." *The Jerusalem Bible* states, "no trace of doubt." *Webster* gives several synonyms, i.e., uncertain, fear, undecided, and suspense. Perhaps the best definition of doubt is questioning. Those whom question God's existence, or God's ability to answer will not receive an answer. God wants you to trust Him then ask Him. That is God's path for answers to prayer.

Lord, I confess my doubts. Forgive me for looking inside to myself, and not looking up to You. I see You in the pages of Scriptures. I hear You in my conscience, and I know Jesus lives in my heart. Forgive me...hear me...please answer. Amen.

One man in Scripture confessed his doubts to Jesus. He said, "Lord, I believe, help my unbelief" (Mark 9:24). This man did not believe demons could be casted out of his possessed son. If you have doubts, begin where the man began, praying, "Lord, I believe." Start with your strength, which is knowing Jesus as Lord. Then focus on what you believe. Now you are ready to ask for help.

Jesus, I come recognizing You are my Lord and my Savior. I believe the Bible and its truth. But Lord about this request , I have doubts...help my unbelief. Teach me what to pray, and give me strength to intercede. Amen.

READING:

Mark 9:14-29

REFLECTION

_____

_____

_____

_____

_____

_____

_____

_____

_____

_____

_____

Day 32

FAITH-PRAYING

"And it is impossible to please God without faith. Anyone who wants to come to him must believe that God exists and that he rewards those who sincerely seek him."

Hebrews 11:6, NLT

FAITH is another condition when asking God for answers to prayer. The verse of the day describes faith with two conditions. First, "must believe that God exist." After all, when you pray to God you must believe He is there to hear you. Second, you must believe. "He rewards those who sincerely seek Him." The first condition is based on recognizing the existence of God. The second condition is based on knowing God can supply and will supply. Therefore, you must approach God in faith, and second you must realize He is both able and willing to give what you ask.

> *Father, I obediently come to You through Jesus Christ as He told me to do. I believe You exist, and You are hearing my petition. So, I ask believing You will be good to me and You are powerful enough to answer my petition. Amen.*

When asking for a big answer to your prayer, i.e., *big* in your opinion. Remember, nothing is too hard for God. You must believe that God is able do it, and that He will do it. "You say to *your* mountain, 'May you be lifted up and thrown into the sea,' and it will happen. But you must really believe it will happen and have no doubt in your heart" (Mark 11:23, NLT). This condition may be the most difficult for humans to follow, because the human heart is deceptive and sinful (Jeremiah 17:9).

Father, I love You with all my heart and I know You exist. Forgive me for my hesitation, it is the doubt in my heart. I ask You to please take away my doubts and teach me to trust You in faith-praying. Amen.

READING:

Hebrews 11:1-10; Mark 11:20-26

REFLECTION

Day 33

IMAGE OF GOD

"And so, dear brothers and sisters, I plead with you to give your bodies to God because of all he has done for you. Let them be a living and holy sacrifice—the kind he will find acceptable. This is truly the way to worship him. Don't copy the behavior and customs of this world, but let God transform you into a new person by changing the way you think. Then you will learn to know God's will for you, which is good and pleasing and perfect."

Romans 12:1-2, NLT

GOD gave you an amazing gift at birth, i.e., God gave you a human body. You have the ethnic and bodily characteristics of your parents. You also have many personality characteristics of your parents, but you are also different in many ways. You also have the characteristics of your Heavenly Father, for "Adam was created a person in the image and likeness of God" (Genesis 2:7). Down through the generations God's image and likeness was transmitted to you. Humans call it personality, i.e., intellect, emotion, will, self-perception, and self-direction. That immaterial personality lives and is expressed in your physical body. You are a complete personality and physical body. God wants your complete person surrendered to Him so He can direct your life and use you in ministry. To let God touch your inner person, yield your body to Him.

Father, I give myself completely to You. Use my feet to guide me. Use my mouth to speak for You. Use my hands to serve You. Fill my mind and heart with Your presence so I can have fellowship with You. Amen.

The real you is immaterial, the real you dwells in your real body. To make sure God gets control of you, the real you in your physical body, you must yield it to God. Letting God guide the outer body is the ultimate way to allowing God to use your inner person. When you give yourself to God, give everything to Him...your inner personality and your outer body.

Father, I begin by giving my total physical being to You. Fill my body with Your presence. Guide my thinking to know You. Accept the worship of my heart as I praise You. Guide my willpower (decision-maker) to seek Your plan for my life. I will do it wholeheartedly. Use me as Your servant. Amen.

READING:

Luke 9:18-62

REFLECTION

Day 34

PLEASING GOD

"Dear friends, you always followed my instructions when I was with you. And now that I am away, it is even more important. Work hard to show the results of your salvation, obeying God with deep reverence and fear. For God is working in you, giving you the desire and the power to do what pleases him."

Philippians 2:12-13, NLT

IF you want God to answer your prayers, try living a life that honors Him by doing those things that please Him. Did you see that phrase in today's verse about pleasing God? When we were born, we learned what it means to please our parents. Then, we learned what it meant to please our spouse, and our children. We ultimately know what it means to please our self. Most think we find life's meaning by pleasing our boss or our self. But the ultimate satisfaction in life is pleasing God. When it comes to prayer, will the answer you seek please God? Maybe there are things in your life that do not please God. What about your attitude? Discipline of time? Use of money? Maybe your prayers are not being answered because something in your life does not please God.

Father, I keep coming with the same prayer requests to please You. I want answers. Are my prayer requests within Your will? Do I have problems relating my Christian testimony to others? Are there hidden sins in my life? I come confessing my weakness and frailty...show me Your plan for my life. Amen.

The Father loves you and sent Jesus to die to take away your sins, you are accepted in His love. Maybe there is something in your life—hidden from you—that is keeping God from answering your prayers.

Lord, I want to please You with my life and actions. Show me anything that displease You and I will confess and seek Your cleansing. I love You and want to serve You. Amen.

READING:

Philippians 2:1-8

REFLECTION

_____

_____

_____

_____

_____

_____

_____

_____

_____

_____

Day 35

IN JESUS' NAME

"You can ask for anything in my name, and I will do it, so that the Son can bring glory to the Father. Yes, ask me for anything in my name, and I will do it!"

John 14:13-14, NLT

IN Matthew 7:7, Jesus told you to ask to get your prayers answered. Now in today's verse Jesus adds a condition to asking. You must ask in Jesus' name. He said, "I will do it." The secret to answered prayers is your relationship to Jesus. You must know Him as Savior from sins, remember your sin blocks your access to the Father in Heaven. Then you must ask because Jesus lives in your life. And you are a shining testimony to others (you don't have hidden sins or mistreat others). Also, your prayer relationship to Jesus means you are reading the Scriptures and growing to be like Him and serving Him in weekly ministry. When Jesus has free access to you and your body, then you can ask and "He will do it."

Jesus, I accepted You as my Savior and You forgave my sins. Now You live in my life and I again yield control to You. Help me be what You want me to be and do what You want me to do. Amen.

When you are rightly related to Jesus, He said you would "bring glory to the Father." The Father is glorified when everyone in Heaven knows and sees your love to the Father. Also, the Father is glorified when you grow spiritually in your inner person. He is also glorified when you are a faithful witness and you minister to others. The Father is glorified when you surrender all to Him and let His influence spread through you.

Father, I yield all to You right now. I want You to be glorified in my life today. Please answer my prayers I make in the name of your Son Jesus. Amen.

READING:

John 14:1-21

REFLECTION

Day 36

ANSWERS TAKE TIME

"Keep on asking, and you will receive what you ask for. Keep on seeking, and you will find. Keep on knocking, and the door will be opened to you. For everyone who asks, receives. Everyone who seeks, finds. And to everyone who knocks, the door will be opened."

Matthew 7:7-8, NLT

DID you see in today's verse that you must keep on asking...seeking...and knocking? Why? God may have many reasons to not answer immediately. Maybe God is at work doing what you ask. If you ask for rain, it may take one or two days for a weather front to deliver rain. If you ask for God to change someone, it may take time for God to send circumstances or someone to change them into what you are requesting. God maybe potentially getting an answer ready for you. Is patience something you might need? If you pray for patience, God won't pour it into your life like filling an empty bottle. No! God will answer by sending circumstances or people to teach you patience.

Father, I do need patience, but it is a hard lesson to learn. Be patient with me. Teach me patience. Teach me patience in prayer. Teach me to pray. Amen.

Remember prayer is a relationship with God. When you are waiting patiently for an answer, maybe God is strengthening your relationship with Him. And when you have a stronger relationship with Him, you can pray with greater faith for the answer. Or, your strengthened relationship with God will prepare you for a "no" answer. Since God has a lot of patience, you are becoming more like Him as you continue in prayer.

Father teach me that my relationship with You is more important than my ability to get answers to prayers. Teach me the most important thing I get from prayer is a strengthened relationship with You. Amen.

READING:

Psalm 42

REFLECTION

Day 37

PRAY IN JESUS' AUTHORITY

"At that time you won't need to ask me for anything. I tell you the truth, you will ask the Father directly, and he will grant your request because you use my name. You haven't done this before. Ask, using my name, and you will receive, and you will have abundant joy."

John 16:23-24, NLT

WHEN you pray using Jesus' name you are using His authority. Remember you don't have access to the Father because you are a sinner (John 8:31). But when you come to the Father in Jesus' authority, He doesn't see your sins, the Father sees the righteousness of Jesus and listens to your requests. Also, as a human you don't know how to ask, the Bible says, "We don't know what God want us to pray for" (Romans 8:26). But when you pray in Jesus' authority, asking in His name, the Father will grant your request because you use My (Jesus) name.

Father, I come to You through the name of Jesus. I ask You to answer my requests because of the authority of Jesus. Be kind to me as You are to Your Son Jesus. Amen.

Answers to prayer don't come because of your merit or even your good Christian life. Also, God does not answer because you pray a long time, or you pray continually. The Father looks on His Son Jesus to answer your requests because you come in the name of Jesus.

Father, I come to You through the authority of Jesus. He is my Savior and Jesus lives in my life. I have yielded my life to Jesus and I want to be a good testimony to friends and others that I am Jesus' disciple. I ask all these things in Jesus name. Amen.

READING:

John 16:19-33

REFLECTION

Day 38

WHEN GOD WAITS

We also pray that you will be strengthened with all his glorious power so you will have all the endurance and patience you need. May you be filled with joy."

Colossians 1:11, NLT

ASK yourself "why doesn't God answer immediately when I ask?" Maybe it is not about the request you seek from God. Maybe God wants to do something else in your life as you wait before Him in prayer. Who knows what weakness God sees in your life that needs strengthening. Obviously, you have many needs, but God who knows all things. He knows what you need now or in the future. He can use your extended time in His presence to strengthen you in one particular area. So, what should you do when the answer does not immediately come? Keep praying... keep yielding...keep waiting...keep knocking.

Father, I love waiting in Your presence. I feel my faith growing stronger in Your presence. Give me faith to get the answers I seek in prayer. Give me patience to continue in prayer. Make me into a prayer-partner with You. Amen.

Look beyond the request you ask from God. Look to God to strengthen your relationship with Him. Look to God to direct your prayer about your present request. Does God want you to change your request...to intensify your faith...or to continue on your present prayer path? One of the wonderful results of waiting in prayer is that it gives you time to examine what you are requesting. It also gives you time to strength your relationship with God.

Father be practical with me, and give me patience to learn to be more patient with everything in life, including being patient with You. Amen.

READING:

1 Kings 19:1-21

REFLECTION

Day 39

FELLOWSHIP TIME

"Our fellowship is with the Father and with his Son, Jesus Christ."

1 John 1:3, NLT

ONE of the wonderful benefits of continuing in prayer is it gives you time for fellowship with God. Are you one of those persons always running into the presence of God with a list of requests? You seek great faith and great patience in prayer to get more results and greater results. That is good, but what about making time to fellowship with God...just enjoying His presence. Yes, you need to give your time to intercession, and to worship, and to praise—but what about fellowship? Learn to just enjoy the Lord and rest in His presence? Don't you fellowship with your spouse and friends? Both you and they need it. What about your fellowship with God?

Lord, I will take time to fellowship with You. I want to know You better. But more than a utilitarian goal of learning facts about You, I want to know You and enjoy fellowshipping with You. The more I enjoy Your presence, the better I can pray and get answers. Amen.

Why would any person fellowship with another? Because of enjoyment! So, you need to seek God's presence, just to enjoy God. And what does enjoyment do? It supports who you are...what you are doing and why. If you enjoy iniquity, you will sin more. If you enjoy God, you will become more godly. So, the more your fellowship with God, the more you will become like Him.

Lord, I enjoy being in Your presence because of what it does for me and to me. Teach me to discipline my time so I can spend it enjoying Your presence and becoming like You. Amen.

READING:

Psalm 27:1-14

REFLECTION

_____

_____

_____

_____

_____

_____

_____

_____

_____

_____

_____

Day 40

THE BEST SPOT

*"As the deer longs for streams of water, so I long for you, O God.
I thirst for God, the living God. When can I go and stand before him?"*

Psalm 42:1-2, NLT

SOME prayers are answered when you pray just once. That is the grace of God. But at other times you will spend time praying in God's presence, you pray for the same request many times. That continued time in God's presence is not wasted time. When you find God's presence, that is the best spot you will ever have in your life. For when you find God, you find out more about yourself. And the more you know of God and yourself, the more peace and enjoyment you will find.

> *Father forgive me for not coming to You more often, and for not staying longer. Also, forgive my selfish inclinations where I do what I want, and I become what I want to be. I yield to You...my time...my ambitions...and the superficial things I do to please myself. Amen.*

Plan to grow your love, joy, peace, and faith. These qualities of life are found in God and His presence. When you first find Jesus, you find forgiveness of sin. Then as you seek to grow in Christian character, you will grow in love, joy, peace, and faith in God's presence. Giving your time to God in prayer is not wasted time, not at all! It is the investment of your time, to grow, love, joy, peace, and faith. Everything that is good is found in God and His presence.

> *Father, I want to love as You love, teach me to give myself to those I want to love. I want a joyful life, teach me the joy of living for You. I surrender to find peace doing Your will. Give me faith as I rest in Your presence. Amen.*

READING:

Psalm 42:1-11

REFLECTION

Day 41

BE STILL

"Wait patiently for the Lord. Be brave and courageous.
Yes, wait patiently for the Lord."

Psalm 27:14, NLT

"Be still in the presence of the Lord and wait patiently for him to act."

Psalm 37:7, NLT

TODAY'S verses challenge you to "wait" or "be still" in the presence of the Lord. The emphasis is not on your inactivity, but on God's presence. It is not what you do—it is where you do it. In your reading, focus on God's presence to see what God will do for you. In your praying, again focus on God's presence to understand what He has for you. Focus on "in His presence," which means being next to God, or facing God. When you are near God, you have found the very best place in life, or in the world. When you are near God, nothing else matters.

Lord, I am not close enough to You. I want to get as close to You as possible to find guidance...peace...energy...positive outlook...protection. I want to get close to You, because of who You are and what You can do for me. Amen.

Today's devotion is in the series of continuous praying. But if you are close to God, you don't have to worry about distance. Turn your face to God and let Him turn His face to you. That is all you want and perhaps that is all you need. Now, you are in the perfect place to pray for answers. You are close enough to God to understand what He wants you to do and become. When there is nothing between God and you, that is the perfect plan in life. Now activate His presence in your life, and become all God designed you to be and do.

Lord, I love being in Your intimate presence. When I know You and realize You know me, I am motivated to serve You and fellowship with You. Amen.

READING:

Psalm 84:1-12

REFLECTION

Day 42

ASK, SEEK, KNOCK

"Keep on asking, and you will receive what you ask for. Keep on seeking, and you will find. Keep on knocking, and the door will be opened to you. For everyone who asks, receives. Everyone who seeks, finds. And to everyone who knocks, the door will be opened."

Matthew 7:7-8, NLT

DID you see a progression in the three verbs in today's verses telling you how to pray? The first verb is *asking*, that is something you request with words from your mouth. When you want or need something, you simply ask for what you need. When asking doesn't get an answer, the next verb is more intentional. You *seek*. That means going to where you will find what you need. Your feet are used involving the whole body. That includes your eyes to look, and your mind to think of where to look. The third verb is *knock*; this is more intentional than the first two commands. When you knock, you use your hand, maybe a doorbell. But this third verb involves going directly to the place where you think you will find your answer. You involve another when you knock on their door.

Father, I come asking for an answer and when it didn't come, I went seeking where I could find my answer. Then I persisted. I began knocking so people would hear me. Father see my need and please give me an answer. Amen.

The first letters of three verbs makes an acronym, i.e., ask...seek...knock = ASK. It directs your heart to ask for the thing for which you are praying. It is said, asking is the rule in God's Kingdom. We must ask...but ask correctly...and ask continuously...and ask as we obey Scriptures...and ask according to the will and plan of God. When you ask, you are obeying Jesus who told you to ask.

Father, I come asking because Jesus told me to ask You for the things, I need in serving You. Also, asking was Jesus' example because He asked You for things. So, I ask because You are my Heavenly Father. Amen.

READING:

Matthew 7:7-12; John 14:2-26

REFLECTION

Day 43

PRAYER MEETINGS

[When Peter was miraculously delivered from prison,] *"he went to the home of Mary...where many were gathered for prayer. He knocked at the door in the gate, and a servant girl named Rhoda...recognized Peter's voice...instead of opening the door, she ran back inside...meanwhile, Peter continued knocking."*

Acts 12:12-16, NLT

TWO observations in today's verses. First, people were praying inside asking God to release Peter from prison but didn't have faith to believe Peter was at the door. Is that an illustration of our lack of faith that God will answer our prayers? Second, Peter had to continue knocking to get into the house, and away from danger. Is Peter's persistence an illustration of our continual praying for the things we want from God? Since we believe God will answer, then we must be like Peter and continue knocking at the door until we get the answer we seek.

Father give me faith to believe in You when I pray. Sometimes I have doubts, so be merciful and forgive my doubts. Give me persistence to keep knocking on the door like Peter so I can get answers to my requests. Amen.

This story is included in Scriptures to encourage us to continue praying, i.e., knocking on Hheaven's door for answers. "While Peter was in prison, the church prayed very earnestly for him" (Acts 12:5). It doesn't say what they were asking for. Were they asking for mercy...deliverance...change in judge's decision...for Peter to have a merciful death? As always, God answered exceeding...abundantly...above all they could ask or think (Eph. 3:20).

Father help me look at answers to my prayers from Your perspective. Give me strong faith when I am weak...give me persistent faith when I want to give up. Give me victorious faith when I look to You for answers. Amen.

READING:

Acts 12:1-19

REFLECTION

Day 44

SHOW GRATITUDE

*"Don't worry about anything; instead, pray about everything. Tell God what you
need, and thank him for all he has done. Then you will experience God's peace,
which exceeds anything we can understand. His peace will guard your
hearts and minds as you live in Christ Jesus."*

Philippians 4:6-7, NLT

D ID you see one secret to answered prayers in today's verse? "Tell God" and "Thank Him.
Does your "thanks" come before or after you ask God? The answer is "both." Before you
ask God for an answer, show gratitude. Why, because God rejoices when His people are
thankful. Then after you pray, thank God for the answer—even before it comes. That is more than
faith-praying. You thank Him because you *want an answer,* and you thank Him because you *know He
will answer.* So, Paul says show appreciation *before* you pray, *during* your prayer, and *after* your pray.

*Lord, I begin my prayers by thanking You for past answers. Then I continue praying giving
thanks that You hear my prayers. Then, I will conclude by thanking You for coming answers.
Amen.*

One more thing about Paul's example of thanks. Go back to the beginning of Philippians. Paul
prayed, "Every time I think of you, I give thanks to my God" (1:3). Now would be a proper time to
thank God for all in your family, then thank God for all who has had a part in your salvation. Finally,
thank God for all you have won to Christ or those who are mentoring.

*Lord, teach me to be grateful for all You have done for me, and for my family, and for my
church and friends. Teach me to live a life of gratitude. Amen.*

READING:

Philippians 4:1-23

REFLECTION

Day 45

THANKING GOD FOR PROBLEMS

"Be thankful in all circumstances, for this is God's will for you."

1 Thessalonians 5:18, NLT

DOES this mean thanking God for problems? Yes...all means all, all of the time! Because life has challenges, thank God for problems. Because other people's sins hurt you, thank God for what you learn and how you have grown. Your friends and family are not perfect, but they may create some problems for you—be thankful. Because you are not perfect, and you have gotten angry or you have created your own problems—be thankful. You don't want to complain and end up in the negative world of complainers—so be thankful.

Lord, get my eyes off my problems, teach me to thank You for all kinds of problems...those that teach me, those that strengthen me, and those that correct me. Teach me to look on the "thankful side" of problems. I don't want to be controlled by my problems. I want to be controlled by You. Amen.

When Paul said, "Be thankful in all circumstances," he didn't make a distinction between good days and bad ones. He didn't make a distinction between easy problems and those that seem to have no solutions. Be thankful that you are alive...and you are God's child...and that you have choices in life...and that you are smart enough to solves problems.

Lord, thank You for all the problems I have solved in the past. Thank You for those You solved, and thank You for what I have learned. Now, get me ready for future problems, because I know they invariably come in life. Amen.

READING:

1 Thessalonians 5:1-28

REFLECTION

Day 46

GOD IS GOOD

"I thank God, whom I serve with a pure conscience, as my forefathers did."

2 Timothy 1:3, NKJV

"Give thanks to the Lord, for He is good!"

Psalm 106:1, NKJV

DON'T just thank God for good things and for answers to prayers. Always focus on Him, and thank God for Himself. It is alright to thank God for good things, and you should always do it. But thank God because He is good. Remember Jesus said, "No one is good... but God" (Matthew 19:17, NKJV). Since children pray before a meal, "God is great God is good" wouldn't that be a good reminder for your prayers. Because God is good, be grateful and thank Him for His goodness.

Lord, You are good to me. You have given me physical life...opportunity...and eternal life. Thank You for being good to me. Help me never forget to be thankful for all the good things You have done for me. Amen.

A friend of mine dedicated three days of his devotional time thanking God for all the good things God had given him. He decided not to ask for anything. For three days he spent his prayer time in continual thanks. He said, "The more I thanked God for His goodness, the more other things I thought of to add to the list." Try it for one daily devotion—thank God for all the good things He has done for you. It will change your prayer life.

Lord, forgive me for selfishness praying only for myself and my needs. I look to Your goodness and I thank You for everything You have given to me. Amen.

READING:

Psalm 100

REFLECTION

_____

_____

_____

_____

_____

_____

_____

_____

_____

_____

Day 47

HARD TIMES

"And we know that God causes everything to work together[a] for the good of those who love God and are called according to his purpose for them."

Romans 8:28, NLT

IT is difficult to praise God in hard times; God will hear your praise and not forget you. James describes these difficulties, "For you know that when your faith is tested, your endurance has a chance to grow" (James 1;3, NLT). So, when problems arise, thank God for an opportunity to grow strong in Christ. Praising God in hard times won't cost you anything. But focusing on bad times and always complaining and criticizing will always pull you down. So, if you thank God in difficulties He will remember, and you will grow in faith. But when you slosh around in the mud of bitterness and complaints, it will only make you dirty.

Lord, it is hard to be grateful when trials come, no one likes difficulties. I don't. But, help me look to Jesus and be grateful for the opportunity to be like Him. I remember His pain and suffering. Amen.

When you look beyond your problems, you will see all the Lord has done for you. First, He gives you eternal life with Him. Second, He forgives all your sins. Third, He justifies you, which means you stand perfect in God's sight. But also, Jesus lives in your heart, gives you peace and joy. On top of it all, you are part of God's family.

Lord, forgive me for complaining, it is the struggles of living in the flesh. Give me peace to accept difficulties. Give me joy to rejoice with You and all other believers. Amen.

READING:

Romans 8:28-39

REFLECTION

Day 48

DIFFICULT DAYS

"I came naked from my mother's womb, and I will be naked when I leave.
The Lord gave me what I had, and the Lord has taken it away.
Praise the name of the Lord!"

Job 1:21-22, NLT

"You intended to harm me, but God intended it all for good. He brought me to
this position so I could save the lives of many people."

Genesis 50:20, NKJV

JOB was able to praise God for his misfortune. When someone criticized him, Job answered, "Should we accept only good things from the hand of God and never anything bad?" So, in all this, Job said nothing wrong." (Job 2:10, NLT). You get God's attention when you praise Him and thank Him for all things—good and bad. That means answered prayers, and those that are not answered. The ability to look beyond yourself to see God working in your life is a mark of spiritual maturity. It may be difficult but look to God anyway.

Lord, I look through my problems, I am looking for Your hand. Show me what You are
doing. Teach me what to do next time. Forgive me for mistakes. Guide me through all the
hurts. Help me rejoice in You and give You thanks for all things. Amen.

When you learn to handle your problems with God, you begin to grow in grace. It is the beginning of learning character. Gratitude is the least remembered of all your virtues by your friends. But showing gratitude is the acid test of character. And remember, "character is habitually doing the right thing, in the right way, at the right time, for the right purpose."

Lord, help me learn gratitude for difficult days, then all the other ones will be easy. Teach me how to handle the problems of life. Amen.

READING:

Job 42:1-16

REFLECTION

Day 49

BLESS THE LORD

"Bless the Lord, O my soul; and all that is within me, bless His holy name!
Bless the Lord, O my soul, and forget not all His benefits."

Psalm 103:1-2, NKJV

REMEMBER, God *gives*, and He *forgives*, so give thanks. When you learn that God is a forgiving God, you will come to Him after you sin, so He will forgive and answer your prayers (1 John 1:9). But also, when you learn about God's forgiveness, you will come quicker. Remember the time you suffered and struggled with your sin problem. The quicker you come asking for forgiveness, the sooner He will forgive. Also, learn to come clean, don't hold back secrets from God. He knows everything (Psalm 139:3-4). If you have not learned the language of gratitude, you are not on speaking terms with God.

> *Lord, forgive me for struggling with my doubts and sins. I confess them to You. And Lord,*
> *I also struggle with problems and trials. Teach me that You forgive soon as I confess. Lord*
> *be merciful to me. Amen.*

If you spend your life looking at your problems, you will be a pessimist. If you spend your life looking at your failures and sins, you will be a quitter. If you spend your life refusing to confess you sins and thank God for cleansing, you will miss out on His blessings.

> *Lord, I come to You as a doubter, I pray like the man in Scriptures, "Lord, I believe, help*
> *my unbelief" (Mark 9:24, NKJV). Lord, I come because I am tired of my doubting and*
> *sinning. Forgive me...cleanse me...Ah! Fellowship with You feels good" Amen.*

READING:

Psalm 103:1-22

REFLECTION

Day 50

THANK YOU

"Jesus lifted up His eyes and said,
'Father, I thank You that You have heard Me.'"

John 11:41

"Jesus...took bread; and when He had given thanks,
He broke it and said, 'Take, eat.'"

1 Corinthians 11:23-24, NKJV

I F you want to be like Jesus, then you will learn to say often, *thank you*. Was Jesus the only one who didn't need to say *thank you* because He was God? Or did Jesus give thanks as a model for us to learn thankfulness? Neither! Jesus gave thanks because that was His nature. Jesus gave thanks because that is what He did. He gave thanks to show appreciation for others who did things for Him. He gave thanks in honest appreciation for those who provided for Him. Jesus gave thanks because it was the right thing to do.

Lord, forgive me for the times I have been ungrateful to my parents and others who provided for me. Forgive me for the times I have been unthankful to You for all that I am, and all I can do. Thank You for my life...my forgiveness...my place in eternal Heaven...and Your fellowship. Amen.

Did you know, we get God's grace for giving thanks? So be grateful (with grace) to those who do for you. But remember, "grace is unexpected, it is the exact opposite of what you deserve." You deserve hell, but grace gives Heaven. You deserve punishment, but grace gives you God's glory. You deserve rejection, but God gives you His fellowship. Give thanks!

Lord, I give You thanks for Your gifts of love and forgiveness. I give You thanks for Your gifts of Christ's indwelling. Thank You Jesus for living in me (Galatians 2:20). Amen.

READING:

1 Corinthians 11:23-24

REFLECTION

PART THREE

7 INDISPENSABLE WORDS FOR EFFECTIVE PRAYER

LESSONS

Lesson 1:

ANSWER KEY

FORGIVENESS AND CLEANSING

"We know that God doesn't listen to sinners, but He is ready to hear those who worship Him and do His will"

(John 9:31, NLT)

"Who may ascend into the hill of the Lord? Or who may stand in His holy place? He who has clean hands and a pure heart, who has not lifted up his soul to an idol, nor sworn deceitfully"

(Psalm 24:3-4).

"Forgive us our sins"

(Matthew 6:12).

A. GETTING READY TO PRAY

1. The key to the Second Great Awakening was a layman's constant prayer. "Lord,...are my hands clean?"

2. Not cleaner than before, God wants a **pure heart**. Righteousness is conforming to God's law; purity is conforming to God's nature.

3. Whatever God's light reveals, Jesus' blood cleanses. But what about secret sins, or **ignorant sins**? "Cleanse your servant from ignorant sins and keep your servant from presumptuous sins" (Psa. 19:12-13, ELT).

4. Old hymn, "What can wash away our sins?" Answer, "Nothing but the blood of Jesus" "The blood... cleanses from all sin" (1 John 1:7).

5. An old saying, "To get completely clean, we must completely confess."

   a. Recognize your **old nature** and rebellion. "I was born a sinner yes, from the moment my mother conceived me" (Psalm 51:5, *NLT*).

   b. Confess any "faults" when you **forget** to do right/good.

   c. Aware that you **fall short**. "If we claim we don't have a sin nature...fool ourselves" (1 John 1:8, *ELT*). "If we claim we haven't sinned even a little...call God a liar" (1 John 1:10, *ELT*).

6. What is confession?

   a. The opposite of **covering** sin, ignoring sin, denying our sin.

   b. Confession means to **agree** with God about this horror of sin.

   c. Confession means to **admit** wrong thinking, wrong desires, wrongdoing. No hiding, no excuses, no justification.

   d. If we have **messed up**, we should fess up.

   e. Confession includes repentance "to turn from sin and turn to God." We must take full responsibility, forsake (**quit**) and **forget** it.

7. What three actions happen with biblical confession? "If we confess our sins, He is faithful and just to forgive us our sins and to cleanse us from all unrighteousness" (1 John 1:9).

   a. God will be faithful to take care of our sin problem. He won't **ignore it**.

   b. To forgive our sins in God's mind is to make the record **straight**.

   c. He will **cleanse**. This involves our record or inclination to sin and our inner heart and thoughts.

R e m e m b e r...

Forgive our sin – gave us His righteousness

Took our **penalty** – bestowed His pardon

Took our shame – shared His smile

Took our **punishment** – gave us His peace

Experienced our death – granted us His life

8. When you pray "Lord, teach us to pray" (Luke 11:1), you are asking:

    a. Give me a deeper **burden** to pray.

    b. Give me a new **vision** of what God can do.

    c. Point out any **problems** that blocks your response.

    d. Shine a light on my **blindness**.

    e. Make sure you **yield** to His will and purpose.

    f. Confess any sin that **blocks** God's work.

    g. Make all requests **grounded** in Scriptural promise.

    h. Step out on **faith** that moves God.

    i. Commit to **continue** requesting.

    j. **Forgive** any sins where you need cleansing.

    k. Join with **Jesus** in approaching the Father.

    l. Add **gratitude and thankfulness** to request.

FORGIVENESS AND CLEANSING

"We know that God doesn't listen to sinners, but He is ready to hear those who worship Him and do His will"

(John 9:31, NLT)

"Who may ascend into the hill of the Lord? Or who may stand in His holy place? He who has clean hands and a pure heart, who has not lifted up his soul to an idol, nor sworn deceitfully"

(Psalm 24:3-4).

"Forgive us our sins"

(Matthew 6:12).

A. GETTING READY TO PRAY

1. The key to the Second Great Awakening was a layman's constant prayer. "Lord,...are my hands clean?"

2. Not cleaner than before, God wants a _____ . Righteousness is conforming to God's law; purity is conforming to God's nature.

3. Whatever God's light reveals, Jesus' blood cleanses. But what about secret sins, or _____ ? "Cleanse your servant from ignorant sins and keep your servant from presumptuous sins" (Psa. 19:12-13, ELT).

4. Old hymn, "What can wash away our sins?" Answer, "Nothing but the blood of Jesus" "The blood… cleanses from all sin" (1 John 1:7).

5. An old saying, "To get completely clean, we must completely confess."

   a. Recognize your _____ and rebellion. "I was born a sinner yes, from the moment my mother conceived me" (Psalm 51:5, *NLT*).

   b. Confess any "faults" when you **forget** to do right/good.

   c. Aware that you _____ . "If we claim we don't have a sin nature…fool ourselves" (1 John 1:8, *ELT*). "If we claim we haven't sinned even a little…call God a liar" (1 John 1:10, ELT).

6. What is confession?

   a. The opposite of _____ sin, ignoring sin, denying our sin.

   b. Confession means to _____ with God about this horror of sin.

   c. Confession means to _____ wrong thinking, wrong desires, wrongdoing. No hiding, no excuses, no justification.

   d. If we have _____ , we should fess up.

   e. Confession includes repentance "to turn from sin and turn to God." We must take full responsibility, forsake (_____) and _____ it.

7. What three actions happen with biblical confession? "If we confess our sins, He is faithful and just to forgive us our sins and to cleanse us from all unrighteousness" (1 John 1:9).

   a. God will be faithful to take care of our sin problem. He won't _____ .

   b. To forgive our sins in God's mind is to make the record _____ .

   c. He will _____ . This involves our record or inclination to sin and our inner heart and thoughts.

R e m e m b e r…

Forgive our sin – gave us His righteousness

Took our _____ – bestowed His pardon

Took our shame – shared His smile

Took our _____ – gave us His peace

Experienced our death – granted us His life

8. When you pray "Lord, teach us to pray" (Luke 11:1), you are asking:

    a.   Give me a deeper _____ to pray.

    b.   Give me a new _____ of what God can do.

    c.   Point out any _____ that blocks your response.

    d.   Shine a light on my _____ .

    e.   Make sure you _____ to His will and purpose.

    f.   Confess any sin that _____ God's work.

    g.   Make all requests _____ in Scriptural promise.

    h.   Step out on _____ that moves God.

    i.   Commit to _____ requesting.

    j.   _____ any sins where you need cleansing.

    k.   Join with _____ in approaching the Father.

    l.   Add _____ to request.

PRAISE AND WORSHIP PRAYER

A. WHY BEGIN PRAYER WITH PRAISE

1. Because Jesus instructed them to begin the Lord's Prayer. "Hallowed be Your name" (Matt. 6:9). Other versions translate this to mean to **honor** His name, to **reverence** His name, to **hold high** His name.

2. Because the psalmist commands you, "Enter...His courts with praise" (Ps. 100:4).

3. Because God alone **deserves it**. "My soul shall make its boast in the Lord" (Ps. 34:2).

4. Because Jesus invited you. "The Father seeks worship" (John 4:23).

5. Because praise is your first honest **response**. "Let the highest praise of God be in their mouth" (Ps. 149:6).

6. Psalms—the central and primary book in the Bible **pulls** praise out of us. "Bless the Lord, O my soul; and all that is within me, bless His holy name" (Ps. 103:1).

B. WHAT IS REAL PRAISE?

1. A sincere acknowledgment of God's **worth or value**. "Praise Him according to His excellency" (Ps. 150:2).

2. A **conviction** that must be expressed. "Worthy is the Lamb" (Rev. 5:12).

3. **Gratitude** of genuine appreciation and recognition.

C. HOW CAN WE EXPRESS OUR SINCERE PRAISE?

1. Words or **shouts** from the mouth/soul. "Let your saints shout for joy" (Ps. 139:9).

2. Social **utterance**, a desire to praise God in the hearing of others.

3. **Sacrifice** – what you yield or give up for God. "Let us continually offer the sacrifices of praise to God" (Heb. 13:5).

4. **Song** of expression of the soul in music, verses, chants, etc. "I will sing a new song to You, O God! I will sing Your praises" (Ps. 144:9, NLT).

5. **Testimony**. "Let the redeemed of the Lord say so" (Ps. 107:2).

6. Mingled with dancing and physical expression of **gratitude**. "Praise His name with dancing" (Ps. 149:3).

7. With **uplifted hands**. "And Ezra blessed the Lord, the great God. And all the people answered, Amen, Amen, with lifting up their hands: and they bowed their heads and worshipped the Lord with their faces to the ground" (Neh. 8:6). Also see (1 Tim. 3:2; Ex. 17:11; Ps. 63:4).

D. THINGS OR REASONS TO PRAISE GOD

1. For God's **majesty**, glory, and magnificent grace. "Let heaven and earth praise Him" (Ps. 69:34).

2. For God's works in **creation**, providence. "All Your works shall praise You" (Ps. 145:10). I pray each morning, "Lord you are Elohim—Creator—I am your creation, use me today."

3. For His **choice of you**, salvation and redemption. "All the people saw him walking and praising God" (Acts 3:8).

4. For His **guidance**, using you, spiritual gifts. "You have been with me from birth; from my mother's womb You have cared for me. No wonder I am always praising You!" (Ps. 71:9).

5. For future Heaven and eternal life with Him. "You heard the word...we are sealed...guaranteed of our possession...to the praise of His glory" (Eph. 1:13-14).

Lesson 2:

QUESTIONS

PRAISE AND WORSHIP PRAYER

A. WHY BEGIN PRAYER WITH PRAISE

1. Because Jesus instructed them to begin the Lord's Prayer. "Hallowed be Your name" (Matt. 6:9). Other versions translate this to mean to _____ His name, to _____ His name, to _____ His name.

2. Because the psalmist commands you, "Enter...His courts with praise" (Ps. 100:4).

3. Because God alone _____ . "My soul shall make its boast in the Lord" (Ps. 34:2).

4. Because Jesus invited you. "The Father seeks worship" (John 4:23).

5. Because praise is your first honest _____ . "Let the highest praise of God be in their mouth" (Ps. 149:6).

6. Psalms—the central and primary book in the Bible _____ praise out of us. "Bless the Lord, O my soul; and all that is within me, bless His holy name" (Ps. 103:1).

B. WHAT IS REAL PRAISE?

1. A sincere acknowledgment of God's _____ . "Praise Him according to His excellency" (Ps. 150:2).

2. A _____ that must be expressed. "Worthy is the Lamb" (Rev. 5:12).

3. _____ of genuine appreciation and recognition.

C. HOW CAN WE EXPRESS OUR SINCERE PRAISE?

1. Words or _____ from the mouth/soul. "Let your saints shout for joy" (Ps. 139:9).

2. Social _____ , a desire to praise God in the hearing of others.

3. _____ – what you yield or give up for God. "Let us continually offer the sacrifices of praise to God" (Heb. 13:5).

4. _____ of expression of the soul in music, verses, chants, etc. "I will sing a new song to You, O God! I will sing Your praises" (Ps. 144:9, NLT).

5. _____ . "Let the redeemed of the Lord say so" (Ps. 107:2).

6. Mingled with dancing and physical expression of _____ . "Praise His name with dancing" (Ps. 149:3).

7. With _____ . "And Ezra blessed the Lord, the great God. And all the people answered, Amen, Amen, with lifting up their hands: and they bowed their heads and worshipped the Lord with their faces to the ground" (Neh. 8:6). Also see (1 Tim. 3:2; Ex. 17:11; Ps. 63:4).

D. THINGS OR REASONS TO PRAISE GOD

1. For God's _____ , glory, and magnificent grace. "Let heaven and earth praise Him" (Ps. 69:34).

2. For God's works in _____ , providence. "All Your works shall praise You" (Ps. 145:10). I pray each morning, "Lord you are Elohim—Creator—I am your creation, use me today."

3. For His _____ , salvation and redemption. "All the people saw him walking and praising God" (Acts 3:8).

4. For His _____ , using you, spiritual gifts. "You have been with me from birth; from my mother's womb You have cared for me. No wonder I am always praising You!" (Ps. 71:9).

5. For future Heaven and eternal life with Him. "You heard the word...we are sealed...guaranteed of our possession...to the praise of His glory" (Eph. 1:13-14).

Lesson 3:

FAITH EXPECTANCY

"And it is impossible to please God without faith. Anyone who wants to come to him must believe that God exists and that he rewards those who sincerely seek him."

Hebrews 11:6, NLT

A. INTRODUCTION:
FAITH MEANS EXPECT AN ANSWER

1. The word *faith* is used five ways in Scriptures:

    a. **Doctrinal** faith, "Denied the faith" (1 Tim. 5:8).

    b. **Saving** faith, a verb "by grace are you saved by faith" (Eph. 2:8).

    c. **Justifying** faith, "We have been made right in God's sight by faith" (Rom. 5:1).

    d. **Indwelling** faith, "I live by the faith of the Son of God" (Gal. 2:20).

    e. **Daily living** faith, "We walk by faith, not by sight" (2 Cor. 5:7).

2. Faith is both active (**verb**) and passive (**noun**). The first is trusting, the second is continual trustworthiness.

3. The words *faith* and *believe* occur over 500 times in Scripture. First you believe in the **Person** of Christ, i.e., God–Man. Second, you believe in His death that **forgave** your sins. Third, your life is changed (**repent**) to obey His command.

B. FAITH THE OPEN DOORWAY OF PRAYER

1. God answers **faith-filled** prayers. "Ask and you will receive" (Matt. 7:7). "Whatever you ask in My name, that I will do" (John 14:13).

2. Faith means you believe/know you will **receive**. "Have faith in God...you can say to the mountains,...be lifted up...and it will happen. But you must really believe it will happen" (Mark 11:22-23).

3. Faith is asking for rain and **carrying an umbrella**.

C. FAITH STEPS TO ANSWERS TO PRAYERS

1. Faith must claim and abide in the promises of God in the Bible. "If you abide in Me, and My words abide in you...ask...receive" (John 15:7).

2. **Obey** Scripture. "We receive...whatever we ask...because we obey" (1 John 3:22, NLT).

3. If it's not faith-praying, it is not **praying**. The disciples could not cast out a demon, they asked why? "Because you don't have enough faith" (Matt. 17:20). If you had faith as small as a mustard seed... nothing would be impossible" (Matt. 17:20-21).

4. Seek God with **all your heart**. "God is a rewarder of those who seek Him" (Heb. 11:6).

5. Your faith pleases God. "He that cometh to God must believe that He is..." (Heb. 11:6). God's greatest **delight** is to be believed.

6. God **desires** you to worship and praise Him. Jesus said, "The Father seeks worship" (John 4:23).

7. Your faith **summons** the presence of God. "You are holy, enthroned on the praises of Israel" (Psalm 22:3, NLT). Where can you find God's presence? Where He is **praised**.

8. Add **thanksgiving** to your prayers. Immediately thank God for the answer. "Pray about everything. Tell God what you need, and thank Him for all He has done" (Phil. 4:6, NLT). "He who forgets the language of thankfulness, doesn't speak God's language of prayer."

9. Faith-praying rejoices your heart to continue asking. The word *bless* means **happy**. "In Thy presence is fullness of joy...pleasure forever more" (Psalm 16:11). Not only you, but God is delighted with our faith (Heb. 11:6).

10. Relationship with God produces **<u>growing</u>** faith to expect more answers. We receive little because we expect little. We receive more when we enjoy more fellowship and intimacy with God. Your faith claims everything God offers in His promises.

Lesson 3:

FAITH EXPECTANCY

"And it is impossible to please God without faith. Anyone who wants to come to him must believe that God exists and that he rewards those who sincerely seek him."

Hebrews 11:6, NLT

A. INTRODUCTION: FAITH MEANS EXPECT AN ANSWER

1. The word *faith* is used five ways in Scriptures:

   a. _____ faith, "Denied the faith" (1 Tim. 5:8).

   b. _____ faith, a verb "by grace are you saved by faith" (Eph. 2:8).

   c. _____ faith, "We have been made right in God's sight by faith" (Rom. 5:1).

   d. _____ faith, "I live by the faith of the Son of God" (Gal. 2:20).

   e. _____ faith, "We walk by faith, not by sight" (2 Cor. 5:7).

2. Faith is both active (_____) and passive (_____). The first is trusting, the second is continual trustworthiness.

3. The words _____ and _____ occur over 500 times in Scripture. First you believe in the _____ of Christ, i.e., God–Man. Second, you believe in His death that _____ your sins. Third, your life is changed (_____) to obey His command.

B. FAITH THE OPEN DOORWAY OF PRAYER

1. God answers _____ prayers. "Ask and you will receive" (Matt. 7:7). "Whatever you ask in My name, that I will do" (John 14:13).

2. Faith means you believe/know you will _____ . "Have faith in God...you can say to the mountains,...be lifted up...and it will happen. But you must really believe it will happen" (Mark 11:22-23).

3. Faith is asking for rain and _____ .

C. FAITH STEPS TO ANSWERS TO PRAYERS

1. Faith must claim and abide in the promises of God in the Bible. "If you abide in Me, and My words abide in you...ask...receive" (John 15:7).

2. _____ Scripture. "We receive...whatever we ask...because we obey" (1 John 3:22, NLT).

3. If it's not faith-praying, it is not _____ . The disciples could not cast out a demon, they asked why? "Because you don't have enough faith" (Matt. 17:20). If you had faith as small as a mustard seed...nothing would be impossible" (Matt. 17:20-21).

4. Seek God with _____ . "God is a rewarder of those who seek Him" (Heb. 11:6).

5. Your faith pleases God. "He that cometh to God must believe that He is..." (Heb. 11:6). God's greatest _____ is to be believed.

6. God _____ you to worship and praise Him. Jesus said, "The Father seeks worship" (John 4:23).

7. Your faith _____ the presence of God. "You are holy, enthroned on the praises of Israel" (Psalm 22:3, NLT). Where can you find God's presence? Where He is _____ .

8. Add _____ to your prayers. Immediately thank God for the answer. "Pray about everything. Tell God what you need, and thank Him for all He has done" (Phil. 4:6, NLT). "He who forgets the language of thankfulness, doesn't speak God's language of prayer."

9. Faith-praying rejoices your heart to continue asking. The word *bless* means _____ . "In Thy presence is fullness of joy...pleasure forever more" (Psalm 16:11). Not only you, but God is delighted with our faith (Hebrews 11:6).

10. Relationship with God produces _____ faith to expect more answers. We receive little because we expect little. We receive more when we enjoy more fellowship and intimacy with God. Your faith claims everything God offers in His promises.

YIELD TO GOD'S WILL

"Thy will be done."

Matthew 6:10

*"Father, if it is Your will, take this cup away from Me;
nevertheless, not My will, but Yours, be done."*

Luke 22:42

"Understanding what the will of the Lord is."

Ephesians 5:17

A. INTRODUCTION: GETTING GOD ON YOUR SIDE

1. A destroying **though**...everything that happens is God's will.

2. A demanding **priority**...the will of God is not automatic.

3. An extraordinary **idea**...you can realize God's will in your life.

4. An incredible **privilege**...God allowing you to cooperate with Him.

5. A transforming **promise**...God aligns Himself with praying saints.

B. INVITATION TO PARTNER WITH GOD

1. Prayer is an essential **ingredient** in God's will and His work.

2. You partner with:

   a. God's **name**.

   b. God's **glory**.

   c. God's **Kingdom**.

   d. God's **power** (the Lord's Prayer, Matthew 6:9-13).

   e. You are implementing God's will on earth, **not yours**. Saul's prayer that turned him into Paul the apostle, "Lord, what will you have me do" (Acts 9:3-6).

   f. How do you enter into a **partnership** with God? "We are partners with Christ when we are steadfast (in prayer)" (Hebrews 3:14, ELT).

C. STEPS TO YIELDING

1. Surrender/yield your **failures**...hurts...doubts...anxiety. "You become the slave of whatever you choose to obey...choose to obey God" (Romans 6:16).

2. Surrender/yield your **selfish desires**...self-glory...self-will...sins. "Do not let your body be an instrument of evil...give yourself completely to God" (Romans 6:13, NLT).

3. Surrender/yield your **bodies**. "Give your bodies to God" (Romans 12:1, NLT).

4. Surrender/yield/seek. Commit to do **God's will.**

   a. God has a **will** (Mark 3:35), which is His desire/choice.

   b. God has a **plan**. "I know the plans I have for you...they are plans for good and not for disaster" (Jeremiah 29:11, NLT).

   c. God has a **goal** for your life and ministry. "For God is working in you, giving you the desire and the power to do what pleases him" (Philippians 2:13, NLT).

Lesson 4:

QUESTIONS

YIELD TO GOD'S WILL

"Thy will be done."

Matthew 6:10

*"Father, if it is Your will, take this cup away from Me;
nevertheless, not My will, but Yours, be done."*

Luke 22:42

"Understanding what the will of the Lord is."

Ephesians 5:17

A. INTRODUCTION: GETTING GOD ON YOUR SIDE

1. A destroying _____ ...everything that happens is God's will.

2. A demanding _____ ...the will of God is not automatic.

3. An extraordinary _____ ...you can realize God's will in your life.

4. An incredible _____ ...God allowing you to cooperate with Him.

5. A transforming _____ ...God aligns Himself with praying saints.

B. INVITATION TO PARTNER WITH GOD

1. Prayer is an essential _____ in God's will and His work.

2. You partner with:

    a. God's _____ .

    b. God's _____ .

    c. God's _____ .

    d. God's _____ (the Lord's Prayer, Matthew 6:9-13).

    e. You are implementing God's will on earth, _____ . Saul's prayer that turned him into Paul the apostle, "Lord, what will you have me do" (Acts 9:3-6).

    f. How do you enter into a _____ with God? "We are partners with Christ when we are steadfast (in prayer)" (Hebrews 3:14, ELT).

C. STEPS TO YIELDING

1. Surrender/yield your _____ ...hurts...doubts...anxiety. "You become the slave of whatever you choose to obey...choose to obey God" (Romans 6:16).

2. Surrender/yield your _____ ...self-glory...self-will...sins. "Do not let your body be an instrument of evil...give yourself completely to God" (Romans 6:13, NLT).

3. Surrender/yield your _____ . "Give your bodies to God" (Romans 12:1, NLT).

4. Surrender/yield/seek. Commit to do _____ .

    a. God has a _____ (Mark 3:35), which is His desire/choice.

    b. God has a _____ . "I know the plans I have for you...they are plans for good and not for disaster" (Jeremiah 29:11, NLT).

    c. God has a _____ for your life and ministry. "For God is working in you, giving you the desire and the power to do what pleases him" (Philippians 2:13, NLT).

Lesson 5:

ASKING: THE PATHWAY TO ANSWERS

A. INTRODUCTION—WHY ASK?

1. Because we are **told**, "Keep on asking and you will receive what you ask" (Matthew 7:7, *NLT*).

2. Because it **works**, "Elijah...prayed earnestly that no rain...none fell" (James 5:17, NLT).

3. Because we **need**. "Ye have not because ye ask not" (James 4:2).

4. Because of **relationship**. "Little children...knows God listens to them" (1 John 4:4-5).

B. THE RULES OF ASKING: MAKING YOUR REQUEST EFFECTIVE BY:

1. His **authority**. "Whatsoever ye shall ask in My name, that will I do" (John 14:13).

2. **Relationship** with the Father. "Ask the Father directly...use My name" (John 16:23, NLT).

3. **Expectantly**. "Ask in faith, nothing wavering" (James 1:6).

4. **Sincerity**. "Anyone who wants to come to Him must believe that God exists" (Hebrews 11:6, NLT).

5. **Continually**. "Keep on asking..." (Matthew 7:7, NLT).

6. **His will**. "This is confidence...if we ask accordingly to His will (1 John 5:14).

7. **Bible**. "If you abide in Me and My words abide in you...ask" (John 15:7).

8. **Obedience**. "We will receive from Him whatever we ask because we obey Him" (1 John 3:22, NLT).

C. HOW TO APPLY THE RULES OF PRAYER

1. Begin with the Lord's Prayer.

2. **Write** out prayer list.

3. Separate your request: importance and **imperative**, i.e., daily and immediate.

4. Write your **responses** on your prayer list.

5. Note items of **praise**.

6. Write and claim prayer **promises**.

7. Include biggest request and not overlook **small request**.

ASKING: THE PATHWAY TO ANSWERS

A. INTRODUCTION—WHY ASK?

1. Because we are _____ , "Keep on asking and you will receive what you ask" (Matthew 7:7, NLT).

2. Because it _____ , "Elijah...prayed earnestly that no rain...none fell" (James 5:17, NLT).

3. Because we _____ . "Ye have not because ye ask not" (James 4:2).

4. Because of _____ . "Little children...know God listens to them" (1 John 4:4-5).

B. THE RULES OF ASKING: MAKING YOUR REQUEST EFFECTIVE BY:

1. His _____ . "Whatsoever ye shall ask in My name, that will I do" (John 14:13).

2. _____ with the Father. "Ask the Father directly...use My name" (John 16:23, NLT).

3. _____ . "Ask in faith, nothing wavering" (James 1:6).

4. _____ . "Anyone who wants to come to Him must believe that God exists" (Hebrews 11:6, NLT).

5. _____ . "Keep on asking..." (Matthew 7:7, NLT).

6. _____ . "This is confidence...if we ask accordingly to His will (1 John 5:14).

7. _____ . "If you abide in Me and My words abide in you...ask" (John 15:7).

8. _____ . "We will receive from Him whatever we ask because we obey Him" (1 John 3:22, NLT).

C. HOW TO APPLY THE RULES OF PRAYER

1. Begin with the Lord's Prayer.

2. _____ out prayer list.

3. Separate your request: importance and _____ , i.e., daily and immediate.

4. Write your _____ on your prayer list.

5. Note items of _____ .

6. Write and claim prayer _____ .

7. Include biggest request and not overlook _____ .

Lesson 6:

KNOCK MORE THAN ONCE

"Keep on asking, and you will receive what you ask for. Keep on seeking, and you will find. Keep on knocking, and the door will be opened to you."

Mathew. 7:7, NLT

A. KNOCK MEANS YOU ANTICIPATE ENTRANCE

1. Definition: To strike a sounding blow, seeking admittance, calling attention, or giving a signal.

2. What is involved in knocking?

   a. Your **initiative** to contact.

   b. Your **signal** to someone.

   c. **Communicating** your desire.

   d. For entrance or **response**.

3. What is prayer?

   a. You initiate a **relationship** with God.

   b. You have a **message** to give to God.

   c. Using communication.

   d. To get response from God.

B. WHAT ABOUT DELIVERANCE

1. The **problem**. "King Herod...persecuted some believers...the apostle James...killed with a sword... arrested Peter...Peter was in prison" (Acts 12:1-2,4).

2. How did the church **pray**? "While Peter was in prison, the church prayed very earnestly for him" (Acts 12:5).

3. God didn't deliver James, but He delivered Peter.

   a. **Secure** in solitary confinement. "Fastened with two chains between two soldiers" (v. 6). "In a cell" (v. 7). "First and second guard post" (v. 10). "Iron gate that led to the city" (v. 10).

   b. Peter slept **soundly**. "Suddenly...a bright light in the cell ...an angel of the Lord struck him on the side to awaken" (v. 7).

   c. **Bondage** released. "The chains fell off" (v. 7).

   d. **Instructed**. "Quick get up" (v. 7). "Get dressed" (v. 8). "Put on your coat" (v. 8).

   e. **Freedom**. "The iron gate...opened...all by itself" (v. 10).

   f. Now **what**? "They passed through and started walking down the street...suddenly the angel left him" (v. 10).

C. WHAT ABOUT THE KNOCKING?

1. Went to Mary's house where the church **prayed**. "He went to the house of Mary...where many were gathered for prayer" (12:12).

2. Went to **Christians**. "Where two or three...I am there" (Matthew 18:20).

3. The act of **obedient** knocking. "He knocked at the door in the gate" (10:13).

4. What did the door represent?

   a. **Fellowship**.

   b. **Safety**.

   c. Acceptance.

   d. God's **answer**.

5. Why didn't Rhoda open the door?

    a. **<u>Excitement</u>**.

    b. Not realize danger.

6. What was the response of those praying?

    a. Unbelief.

    b. **<u>Doubt</u>**.

    c. Belief in Herod's **<u>justice</u>**.

    d. **<u>Doubted</u>** an answered prayer.

    e. Believed the worst, i.e., Peter was dead (angel).

7. What was the greatest act of **<u>obedience</u>**? "Peter continued knocking" (v. 16).

8. **<u>Response</u>**:

    a. "They were amazed" (v. 16).

    b. Testing. "He told them" (v. 17).

    c. "Go tell (other) James" (v. 17).

<h1 style="text-align:center">Lesson 6:</h1>

KNOCK MORE THAN ONCE

*"Keep on asking, and you will receive what you ask for.
Keep on seeking, and you will find. Keep on
knocking, and the door will be opened to you."*

Mathew. 7:7, NLT

A. KNOCK MEANS YOU ANTICIPATE ENTRANCE

1. Definition: To strike a sounding blow, seeking admittance, calling attention, or giving a signal.

2. What is involved in knocking?

    a. Your _____ to contact.

    b. Your _____ to someone.

    c. _____ your desire.

    d. For entrance or _____ .

3. What is prayer?

    a. You initiate a _____ with God.

    b. You have a _____ to give to God.

    c. Using communication.

    d. To get response from God.

B. WHAT ABOUT DELIVERANCE

1. The _____ . "King Herod...persecuted some believers...the apostle James...killed with a sword...arrested Peter...Peter was in prison" (Acts 12:1-2,4).

2. How did the church _____ ? "While Peter was in prison, the church prayed very earnestly for him" (Acts 12:5).

3. God didn't deliver James, but He delivered Peter.

   a. _____ in solitary confinement. "Fastened with two chains between two soldiers" (v. 6). "In a cell" (v. 7). "First and second guard post" (v. 10). "Iron gate that led to the city" (v. 10).

   b. Peter slept _____ . "Suddenly...a bright light in the cell ...an angel of the Lord struck him on the side to awaken" (v. 7).

   c. _____ released. "The chains fell off" (v. 7).

   d. _____ . "Quick get up" (v. 7). "Get dressed" (v. 8). "Put on your coat" (v. 8).

   e. _____ . "The iron gate...opened...all by itself" (v. 10).

   f. Now _____ ? "They passed through and started walking down the street...suddenly the angel left him" (v. 10).

C. WHAT ABOUT THE KNOCKING?

1. Went to Mary's house where the church _____ . "He went to the house of Mary...where many were gathered for prayer" (12:12).

2. Went to _____ . "Where two or three...I am there" (Matthew 18:20).

3. The act of _____ knocking. "He knocked at the door in the gate" (10:13).

4. What did the door represent?

   a. _____ .

   b. _____ .

   c. Acceptance.

   d. God's _____ .

5. Why didn't Rhoda open the door?

    a. _____ .

    b. Not realize danger.

6. What was the response of those praying?

    a. Unbelief.

    b. _____ .

    c. Belief in Herod's _____ .

    d. _____ an answered prayer.

    e. Believed the worst, i.e., Peter was dead (angel).

7. What was the greatest act of _____ ? "Peter continued knocking" (v. 16).

8. _____ :

    a. "They were amazed" (v. 16).

    b. Testing. "He told them" (v. 17).

    c. "Go tell (other) James" (v. 17).

AN ATTITUDE OF GRATITUDE

A. INTRODUCTION

1. My high school World Literature class. "Gratitude is the least remembered of all virtues and is the acid test of **character**." Character is defined "Habitually doing the right thing, in the right way, for the right purpose."

2. Do you take things for granted, or take things with **gratitude**?

3. Don't add up your troubles but **count your blessings**.

4. Gratitude is one of the nine Fruit of the Spirit. "Love, joy, peace, patience, kindness, goodness, faithfulness, gentleness and self-control" (Gal. 5:22, NLT). The word joy is *xara* "outward expression of thanksgiving to God." Joy is not something you get from outward pleasure or things. True joy comes from doing or saying the right things.

5. Gratitude (history).

    a. Expression of **appreciation** given without being asked.

    b. Given without force or demand, i.e., apology.

    c. Not expecting **additional return**.

    d. Not called for by circumstance.

    e. The word *gratitude* is not found in the **King James**. Synonym, i.e., thanks, thankfulness.

B. GRATITUDE AND THANKFULNESS IN SCRIPTURES

1. Gratitude/thank in initial **approach** to God. "Be thankful unto Him and bless His name" (Psalm 100:4).

2. Gratitude/thanks is a **sacrifice** (something you don't have to give). "I will offer Thee the sacrifice of thanksgiving" (Psalm 116:17).

3. Jesus gave thanks. "I thank Thee that Thou hast heard Me" (John 11:41).

4. Jesus gave thanks for the bread and cup (Matthew 26:26-27).

5. Paul thanked God for his **memory** of young believers (Phil. 1:3).

6. Paul instructed to add gratitude/thankfulness to prayers (Phil. 4:6).

C. PRINCIPLES TO GROW GRATITUDE

1. Don't fall for the trap to be thankful only when you feel like it. **No**! When you are grateful or thankful from your **character**, you will change your expectations, i.e., you will change your life.

2. Practice gratitude so your emotions will catch up with your **attitude**.

3. Don't just thank God for good things—thank Him because **He is good**.

4. Job praised God in misfortune—the bases for **return blessings**. "I came naked from my mother's womb, and I will be naked when I leave. The Lord gave me what I had, and the Lord has taken it away. Praise the name of the Lord!" (Job 1:21, NLT).

5. Praising God in hard times won't **cost you anything**, God will see and remember, but focusing on bad things and complaining and criticizing will always **pull you down to their level**.

6. Look beyond your circumstance to what you have, i.e., forgiveness, justification, accepted, **eternal life**.

7. Remember, God **gives**, and He **forgives**, so give thanks.

8. "If you haven't learned the language of gratitude, you are not on speaking terms with God."

9. Harold Vaughan went three days with a *Gratitude of Thanksgiving* in prayer, vowing to not make a request or ask for anything for three days. "The longer I thanked God, the more I realized how fortunate I was."

10. "In everything give thanks" (1 Thess. 5:18). Does this mean thanking God for problems? Does Paul make any distinction between good days and bad days?

11. Always remember what you were before God found you and **saved you**.

12. If you spend your life looking for the dark...the mistakes...the sins...the people who hurt you...you will find them and **lots more**.

D. 7 GRATEFUL STEPS TO OVERCOME OBSTACLES AND EVIL

1. **Pray**. "Pray for them which despitefully use you" (Luke 6:28).

2. **Do right**. "Do to others as you would like them to do to you" (Luke 6:31).

3. **Testimony**. "...truly be acting as children of the Most High, for he is kind to those who are unthankful and wicked" (Luke 6:35, NLT).

4. **Do good**. "Recompense no one evil for evil" (Romans 12:14).

5. **Forget**. "average not yourselves" (Roman 12:19).

6. **Give them to God**. "I will pay them back, says the Lord" (Romans 12:19).

7. Conquer **evil with good**. "Overcome evil with good" (Romans 12:21).

Lesson 7:

QUESTIONS

AN ATTITUDE OF GRATITUDE

A. INTRODUCTION

1. My high school World Literature class. "Gratitude is the least remembered of all virtues and is the acid test of _____." Character is defined "Habitually doing the right thing, in the right way, for the right purpose."

2. Do you take things for granted, or take things with _____?

3. Don't add up your troubles but _____.

4. Gratitude is one of the nine Fruits of the Spirit. "Love, joy, peace, patience, kindness, goodness, faithfulness, gentleness and self-control" (Gal. 5:22, NLT). The word joy is *xara* "outward expression of thanksgiving to God." Joy is not something you get from outward pleasure or things. True joy comes from doing or saying the right things.

5. Gratitude (history).

   a. Expression of _____ given without being asked.

   b. Given without force or demand, i.e., apology.

   c. Not expecting _____.

   d. Not called for by circumstance.

   e. The word *gratitude* is not found in the _____. Synonym, i.e., thanks, thankfulness.

B. GRATITUDE AND THANKFULNESS IN SCRIPTURES

1. Gratitude/thank in initial _____ to God. "Be thankful unto Him and bless His name" (Psalm 100:4).

2. Gratitude/thanks is a _____ (something you don't have to give). "I will offer Thee the sacrifice of thanksgiving" (Psalm 116:17).

3. Jesus gave thanks. "I thank Thee that Thou hast heard Me" (John 11:41).

4. Jesus gave thanks for the bread and cup (Matthew 26:26-27).

5. Paul thanked God for his _____ of young believers (Phil. 1:3).

6. Paul instructed to add gratitude/thankfulness to prayers (Phil. 4:6).

C. PRINCIPLES TO GROW GRATITUDE

1. Don't fall for the trap to be thankful only when you feel like it. _____ ! When you are grateful or thankful from your **character**, you will change your expectations, i.e., you will change your life.

2. Practice gratitude so your emotions will catch up with you _____ .

3. Don't just thank God for good things—thank Him because _____ .

4. Job praised God in misfortune—the bases for _____ . "I came naked from my mother's womb, and I will be naked when I leave. The Lord gave me what I had, and the Lord has taken it away. Praise the name of the Lord!" (Job 1:21, NLT).

5. Praising God in hard times won't _____ , God will see and remember, but focusing on bad things and complaining and criticizing will always _____ .

6. Look beyond your circumstance to what you have, i.e., forgiveness, justification, accepted, _____ .

7. Remember, God _____ , and He _____ , so give thanks.

8. "If you haven't learned the language of gratitude, you are not on speaking terms with God."

9. Harold Vaughan went three days with a *Gratitude of Thanksgiving* in prayer, vowing to not make a request or ask for anything for three days. "The longer I thanked God, the more I realized how fortunate I was."

10. "In everything give thanks" (1 Thess. 5:18). Does this mean thanking God for problems? Does Paul make any distinction between good days and bad days?

11. Always remember what you were before God found you and _____ .

12. If you spend your life looking for the dark...the mistakes...the sins...the people who hurt you...you will find them and _____ .

D. 7 GRATEFUL STEPS TO OVERCOME OBSTACLES AND EVIL

1. _____ . "Pray for them which despitefully use you" (Luke 6:28).

2. _____ . "Do to others as you would like them to do to you" (Luke 6:31).

3. _____ . "...truly be acting as children of the Most High, for he is kind to those who are unthankful and wicked" (Luke 6:35, NLT).

4. _____ . "Recompense no one evil for evil" (Romans 12:14).

5. _____ . "average not yourselves" (Roman 12:19).

6. _____ . "I will pay them back, says the Lord" (Romans 12:19).

7. Conquer _____ . "Overcome evil with good" (Romans 12:21).

PART FOUR

7 INDISPENSABLE WORDS
FOR EFFECTIVE PRAYER

POWERPOINT GUIDE

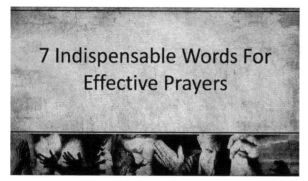

7 Indispensable Words For Effective Prayers

Lesson 1
Forgiveness and Cleansing

"We know that God doesn't listen to sinners, but He is ready to hear those who worship Him and do His will."
John 9:31, NLT

"Who may ascend into the hill of the Lord? Or who may stand in His holy place? He who has clean hands and a pure heart, who has not lifted up his soul to an idol, nor sworn deceitfully."
Psalm 24:3-4

"Forgive us our sins."
Matthew 6:12

A. GETTING READY TO PRAY

1. The key to the Second Great Awakening was a layman's constant prayer. "Lord, . . . are my hands clean?"

2. Not cleaner than before, God wants a <u>pure heart</u>. Righteousness is conforming to God's law; purity is conforming to God's nature.

3. Whatever God's light reveals, Jesus' blood cleanses. But what about secret sins, or <u>ignorant sins</u>? "Cleanse your servant from ignorant sins and keep your servant from presumptuous sins" (Psa. 19:12-13, *ELT*).

4. Old hymn, "What can wash away our sins?" Answer, "Nothing but the blood of Jesus" "The blood . . . cleanses from all sin" (1 John 1:7).

5. An old saying, "To get completely clean, we must completely confess."
   a. Recognize your <u>old nature</u> and rebellion. "I was born a sinner yes, from the moment my mother conceived me" (Psalm 51:5, *NLT*).
   b. Confess any "faults" when you <u>forget</u> to do right/good.
   c. Aware that you <u>fall short</u>. "If we claim we don't have a sin nature . . . fool ourselves" (1 John 1:8, *ELT*). "If we claim we haven't sinned even a little . . . call God a liar" (1 John 1:10, *ELT*).

6. What is confession?
   a. The opposite of <u>covering</u> sin, ignoring sin, denying our sin.
   b. Confession means to <u>agree</u> with God about this horror of sin.
   c. Confession means to <u>admit</u> wrong thinking, wrong desires, wrongdoing. No hiding, no excuses, no justification.
   d. If we have <u>messed up</u>, we should fess up.
   e. Confession includes repentance "to turn from sin and turn to God." We must take full responsibility, forsake (<u>quit</u>) and <u>forget</u> it.

7. What three actions happen with biblical confession? "If we confess our sins, He is faithful and just to forgive us our sins and to cleanse us from all unrighteousness" (1 John 1:9).
   a. God will be faithful to take care of our sin problem. He won't <u>ignore it</u>.
   b. To forgive our sins in God's mind is to make the record <u>straight</u>.
   c. He will <u>cleanse</u>. This involves our record or inclination to sin and our inner heart and thoughts.

Remember …

Forgive our sin – gave us His righteousness
Took our <u>penalty</u> – bestowed His pardon
Took our shame – shared His smile
Took our <u>punishment</u> – gave us His peace
Experienced our death – granted us His life

Slide 9 of 76

8. When you pray "Lord, teach us to pray" (Luke 11:1), you are asking:
   a. Give me a deeper <u>burden</u> to pray.
   b. Give me a new <u>vision</u> of what God can do.
   c. Point out any <u>problems</u> that blocks your response.
   d. Shine a light on my <u>blindness</u>.
   e. Make sure you <u>yield</u> to His will and purpose.

Slide 10 of 76

f. Confess any sin that <u>blocks</u> God's work.
g. Make all requests <u>grounded</u> in Scriptural promise.
h. Step out on <u>faith</u> that moves God.
i. Commit to <u>continue</u> requesting.
j. <u>Forgive</u> any sins where you need cleansing.
k. Join with <u>Jesus</u> in approaching the Father.
l. Add <u>gratitude and thankfulness</u> to request.

Slide 11 of 76

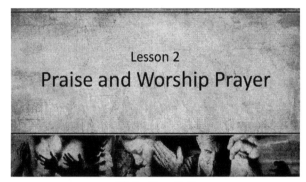

Lesson 2
Praise and Worship Prayer

Slide 12 of 76

A. WHY BEGIN PRAYER WITH PRAISE

1. Because Jesus instructed them to begin the Lord's Prayer. "Hallowed be Your name" (Matt. 6:9). Other versions translate this to mean to <u>honor</u> His name, to <u>reverence</u> His name, to <u>hold high</u> His name.

2. Because the psalmist commands you, "Enter . . . His courts with praise" (Ps. 100:4).

Slide 13 of 76

3. Because God alone <u>deserves it</u>. "My soul shall make its boast in the Lord" (Ps. 34:2).

4. Because Jesus invited you. "The Father seeks worship" (John 4:23).

Slide 14 of 76

5. Because praise is your first honest <u>response</u>. "Let the highest praise of God be in their mouth" (Ps. 149:6).

6. Psalms – the central and primary book in the Bible <u>pulls</u> praise out of us. "Bless the Lord, O my soul; and all that is within me, bless His holy name" (Ps. 103:1).

Slide 15 of 76

B. WHAT IS REAL PRAISE?

1. A sincere acknowledgement of God's <u>worth or value</u>. "Praise Him according to His excellency" (Ps. 150:2).
2. A <u>conviction</u> that must be expressed. "Worthy is the Lamb" (Rev. 5:12).
3. <u>Gratitude</u> of genuine appreciation and recognition.

Slide 16 of 76

C. HOW CAN WE EXPRESS OUR SINCERE PRAISE?

1. Words or <u>shouts</u> from the mouth/soul. "Let your saints shout for joy" (Ps. 139:9).
2. Social <u>utterance</u>, a desire to praise God in the hearing of others.
3. <u>Sacrifice</u> – what you yield or give up for God. "Let us continually offer the sacrifices of praise to God" (Heb. 13:5).

4. <u>Song</u> of expression of the soul in music, verses, chants, etc. "I will sing a new song to You, O God! I will sing Your praises" (Ps. 144:9, *NLT*).

5. <u>Testimony</u>. "Let the redeemed of the Lord say so" (Ps. 107:2).

6. Mingled with dancing and physical expression of <u>gratitude</u>. "Praise His name with dancing" (Ps. 149:3).

7. With <u>uplifted hands</u>. "And Ezra blessed the Lord, the great God. And all the people answered, Amen, Amen, with lifting up their hands: and they bowed their heads and worshipped the Lord with their faces to the ground" (Neh. 8:6). Also see (1 Tim. 3:2; Ex. 17:11; Ps. 63:4).

D. THINGS OR REASONS TO PRAISE GOD

1. For God's <u>majesty</u>, glory, and magnificent grace. "Let heaven and earth praise Him" (Ps. 69:34).

2. For God's works in <u>creation</u>, providence. "All Your works shall praise You" (Ps. 145:10). I pray each morning, "Lord you are Elohim – Creator – I am your creation, use me today."

3. For His <u>choice of you</u>, salvation and redemption. "All the people saw him walking and praising God" (Acts 3:8).

4. For His <u>guidance</u>, using you, spiritual gifts. "You have been with me from birth; from my mother's womb You have cared for me. No wonder I am always praising You!" (Ps. 71:9).

5. For future heaven and eternal life with Him. "You heard the word . . . we are sealed . . . guaranteed of our possession . . . to the praise of His glory" (Eph. 1:13-14).

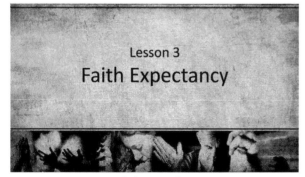

Lesson 3
Faith Expectancy

"And it is impossible to please God without faith. Anyone who wants to come to him must believe that God exists and that he rewards those who sincerely seek him."
Hebrews 11:6, NLT

A. INTRODUCTION: FAITH MEANS EXPECT AN ANSWER

1. The word *faith* is used five ways in Scriptures:
   a. Doctrinal faith, "Denied the faith" (1 Tim. 5:8).
   b. Saving faith, a verb "by grace are you saved by faith" (Eph. 2:8).
   c. Justifying faith, "We have been made right in God's sight by faith" (Rom. 5:1).
   d. Indwelling faith, "I live by the faith of the Son of God" (Gal. 2:20).
   e. Daily living faith, "We walk by faith, not by sight" (2 Cor. 5:7).

2. Faith is both active (verb) and passive (noun). The first is trusting, the second is continual trustworthiness.

3. The words *faith* and *believe* occur over 500 times in Scripture. First you believe in the Person of Christ, i.e., God-Man. Second, you believe in His death that forgave your sins. Third, your life is changed (repent) to obey His command.

B. FAITH THE OPEN DOORWAY OF PRAYER

1. God answers faith-filled prayers. "Ask and you will receive" (Matt. 7:7). "Whatever you ask in My name, that I will do" (John 14:13).

2. Faith means you believe/know you will receive. "Have faith in God . . . you can say to the mountains, . . . be lifted up . . . and it will happen. But you must really believe it will happen" (Mark 11:22-23).

3. Faith is asking for rain and carrying an umbrella.

C. FAITH STEPS TO ANSWERS TO PRAYERS

1. Faith must claim and abide in the promises of God in the Bible. "If you abide in Me, and My words abide in you . . . ask . . . receive" (John 15:7).

2. Obey Scripture. "We receive . . . whatever we ask . . . because we obey" (1 John 3:22, *NLT*).

3. If it's not faith-praying, it is not praying. The disciples could not cast out a demon, they asked why? "Because you don't have enough faith" (Matt. 17:20). If you had faith as small as a mustard seed . . . nothing would be impossible" (Matt. 17:20-21).

4. Seek God with all your heart. "God is a rewarder of those who seek Him" (Heb. 11:6).

5. Your faith pleases God. "He that cometh to God must believe that He is . . ." (Heb. 11:6). God's greatest delight is to be believed.

6. God desires you to worship and praise Him. Jesus said, "The Father seeks worship" (John 4:23).

7. Your faith summons the presence of God. "You are holy, enthroned on the praises of Israel" (Psalm 22:3, *NLT*). Where can you find God's presence? Where He is praised.

8. Add thanksgiving to your prayers. Immediately thank God for the answer. "Pray about everything. Tell God what you need, and thank Him for all He has done" (Phil. 4:6, *NLT*). "He who forgets the language of thankfulness, doesn't speak God's language of prayer."

9. Faith-praying rejoices your heart to continue asking. The word *bless* means <u>happy</u>. "In Thy presence is fullness of joy . . . pleasure forever more" (Psalm 16:11). Not only you, but God is delighted with our faith (Hebrews 11:6).

10. Relationship with God produces <u>growing</u> faith to expect more answers. We receive little because we expect little. We receive more when we enjoy more fellowship and intimacy with God. Your faith claims everything God offers in His promises.

Slide 33 of 76

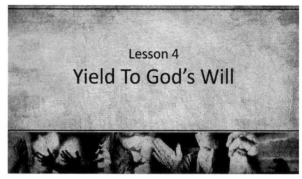

Lesson 4
Yield To God's Will

Slide 34 of 76

"Thy will be done."
Matthew 6:10

"Father, if it is Your will, take this cup away from Me; nevertheless, not My will, but Yours, be done."
Luke 22:42

"Understanding what the will of the Lord is."
Ephesians 5:17

Slide 35 of 76

A. INTRODUCTION: GETTING GOD ON YOUR SIDE

1. A destroying <u>though</u> . . . everything that happens is God's will.

2. A demanding <u>priority</u> . . . the will of God is not automatic.

Slide 36 of 76

3. An extraordinary <u>idea</u> . . . you can realize God's will in your life.

4. An incredible <u>privilege</u> . . . God allowing you to cooperate with Him.

5. A transforming <u>promise</u> . . . God aligns Himself with praying saints.

Slide 37 of 76

B. INVITATION TO PARTNER WITH GOD

1. Prayer is an essential <u>ingredient</u> in God's will and His work.

2. You partner with:
   a. God's <u>name</u>.
   b. God's <u>glory</u>.
   c. God's <u>kingdom</u>.
   d. God's <u>power</u> (the Lord's Prayer, Matthew 6:9-13).

Slide 38 of 76

3. You are implementing God's will on earth, <u>not yours</u>. Saul's prayer that turned him into Paul the apostle, "Lord, what will you have me do" (Acts 9:3-6).

4. How do you enter into a <u>partnership</u> with God? "We are partners with Christ when we are steadfast (in prayer)" (Hebrews 3:14, *ELT*).

Slide 39 of 76

C. STEPS TO YIELDING

1. Surrender/yield your <u>failures</u> . . . hurts . . . doubts . . . anxiety. "You become the slave of whatever you choose to obey . . . choose to obey God" (Romans 6:16).

2. Surrender/yield your <u>selfish desires</u> . . . self-glory . . . self-will . . . sins. "Do not let your body be an instrument of evil . . . give yourself completely to God" (Romans 6:13, *NLT*).

Slide 40 of 76

3. Surrender/yield your <u>bodies</u>. "Give your bodies to God" (Romans 12:1, *NLT*).

4. Surrender/yield/seek. Commit to do <u>God's will</u>.
   a. God has a <u>will</u> (Mark 3:35), which is His desire/choice.
   b. God has a <u>plan</u>. "I know the plans I have for you . . . they are plans for good and not for disaster" (Jeremiah 29:11, *NLT*).
   c. God has a <u>goal</u> for your life and ministry. "For God is working in you, giving you the desire and the power to do what pleases him" (Philippians 2:13, *NLT*).

Slide 41 of 76

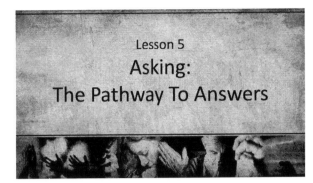

Lesson 5
Asking:
The Pathway To Answers

Slide 42 of 76

A. INTRODUCTION – WHY ASK?

1. Because we are <u>told</u>, "Keep on asking and you will receive what you ask" (Matthew 7:7, *NLT*).

2. Because it <u>works</u>, "Elijah . . . prayed earnestly that no rain . . . none fell" (James 5:17, *NLT*).

Slide 43 of 76

3. Because we <u>need</u>. "Ye have not because ye ask not" (James 4:2).

4. Because of <u>relationship</u>. "Little children . . . knows God listens to them" (1 John 4:4-5).

Slide 44 of 76

B. THE RULES OF ASKING: MAKING YOUR REQUEST EFFECTIVE BY:

1. His <u>authority</u>. "Whatsoever ye shall ask in My name, that will I do" (John 14:13).

2. <u>Relationship</u> with the Father. "Ask the Father directly . . . use My name" (John 16:23, *NLT*).

Slide 45 of 76

3. <u>Expectantly</u>. "Ask in faith, nothing wavering" (James 1:6).

4. <u>Sincerity</u>. "Anyone who wants to come to Him must believe that God exists" (Hebrews 11:6, *NLT*).

5. <u>Continually</u>. "Keep on asking . . ." (Matthew 7:7, *NLT*).

Slide 46 of 76

6. <u>His will</u>. "This is confidence . . . if we ask accordingly to His will (1 John 5:14).

7. <u>Bible</u>. "If you abide in Me and My words abide in you . . . ask" (John 15:7).

8. <u>Obedience</u>. "We will receive from Him whatever we ask because we obey Him" (1 John 3:22, *NLT*).

Slide 47 of 76

C. HOW TO APPLY THE RULES OF PRAYER

1. Begin with The Lord's Prayer.

2. <u>Write</u> out prayer list

3. Separate your request: importance and <u>imperative</u>, i.e., daily and immediate.

Slide 48 of 76

4. Write your responses on your prayer list.

5. Note items of praise.

6. Write and claim prayer promises.

7. Include biggest request and not overlook small request

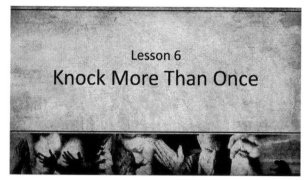

"Keep on asking, and you will receive what you ask for. Keep on seeking, and you will find. Keep on knocking, and the door will be opened to you."
Mathew. 7:7, NLT

A. KNOCK MEANS YOU ANTICIPATE ENTRANCE

1. Definition: To strike a sounding blow, seeking admittance, calling attention or giving a signal.

2. What is involved in knocking?
   a. Your initiative to contact.
   b. Your signal to someone.
   c. Communicating your desire.
   d. For entrance or response.

3. What is prayer?
   a. You initiate a relationship with God.
   b. You have a message to give to God.
   c. Using communication.
   d. To get response from God.

B. WHAT ABOUT DELIVERANCE

1. The problem. "King Herod . . . persecuted some believers . . . the apostle James . . . killed with a sword . . . arrested Peter . . . Peter was in prison" (Acts 12:1-2,4).

2. How did the church pray? "While Peter was in prison, the church prayed very earnestly for him" (Acts 12:5).

3. God didn't deliver James, but He delivered Peter.
   a. Secure in solitary confinement. "Fastened with two chains between two soldiers" (v. 6). "In a cell" (v. 7). "First and second guard post" (v. 10). "Iron gate that led to the city" (v. 10).
   b. Peter slept soundly. "Suddenly . . . a bright light in the cell . . . an angel of the Lord struck him on the side to awaken" (v. 7).

c. <u>Bondage</u> released. "The chains fell off" (v. 7).

d. <u>Instructed</u>. "Quick get up" (v. 7). "Get dressed" (v. 8). "Put on your coat" (v. 8).

e. <u>Freedom</u>. "The iron gate . . . opened . . . all by itself" (v. 10).

f. Now <u>what</u>? "They passed through and started walking down the street . . . suddenly the angel left him" (v. 10).

Slide 57 of 76

C. WHAT ABOUT THE KNOCKING?

1. Went to Mary's house where the church <u>prayed</u>. "He went to the house of Mary . . . where many were gathered for prayer" (12:12).

2. Went to <u>Christians</u>. "Where two or three . . . I am there" (Matthew 18:20).

3. The act of <u>obedient</u> knocking. "He knocked at the door in the gate" (10:13).

Slide 58 of 76

---

4. What did the door represent?
   a. <u>Fellowship</u>.
   b. <u>Safety</u>.
   c. Acceptance.
   d. God's <u>answer</u>.

5. Why didn't Rhoda open the door?
   a. <u>Excitement</u>.
   b. Not realize danger.

Slide 59 of 76

---

6. What was the response of those praying?
   a. Unbelief.
   b. <u>Doubt</u>.
   c. Belief in Herod's <u>justice</u>.
   d. <u>Doubted</u> an answer prayer.
   e. Believed the worst, i.e., Peter was dead (angel).

Slide 60 of 76

---

7. What was greatest act of <u>obedience</u>? "Peter continued knocking" (v. 16).

8. <u>Response</u>:
   a. "They were amazed" (v. 16).
   b. Testing. "He told them" (v. 17).
   c. "Go tell (other) James" (v. 17).

Slide 61 of 76

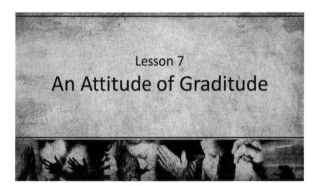

Lesson 7
An Attitude of Graditude

Slide 62 of 76

A. INTRODUCTION

1. My high school World Literature class. "Gratitude is the least remembered of all virtues and is the acid test of <u>character</u>." Character is defined "Habitually doing the right thing, in the right way, for the right purpose."

Slide 63 of 76

---

2. Do you take things for granted, or take things with <u>gratitude</u>?

3. Don't add up your troubles but <u>count your blessings</u>.

Slide 64 of 76

---

4. Gratitude is one of the nine Fruits of the Spirit. "Love, joy, peace, patience, kindness, goodness, faithfulness, gentleness and self-control" (Gal. 5:22, *NLT*). The word joy is *xara* "outward expression of thanksgiving to God." Joy is not something you get from outward pleasure or things. True joy comes from doing or saying the right things.

5. Gratitude (history).
   a. Expression of appreciation given without being asked.
   b. Given without force or demand, i.e., apology.
   c. Not expecting additional return.
   d. Not called for by circumstance.
   e. The word *gratitude* is not found in the King James. Synonym, i.e., thanks, thankfulness.

B. GRATITUDE AND THANKFULNESS IN SCRIPTURES

1. Gratitude/thank in initial approach to God. "Be thankful unto Him and bless His name" (Psalm 100:4).

2. Gratitude/thanks is a sacrifice (something you don't have to give). "I will offer Thee the sacrifice of thanksgiving" (Psalm 116:17).

3. Jesus gave thanks. "I thank Thee that Thou hast heard Me" (John 11:41).

4. Jesus gave thanks for the bread and cup (Matthew 26:26-27).

5. Paul thanked God for his memory of young believers (Phil. 1:3).

6. Paul instructed to add gratitude/thankfulness to prayers (Phil. 4:6).

C. PRINCIPLES TO GROW GRATITUDE

1. Don't fall for trap to be thankful only when you feel like it. No! When you are grateful or thankful from your character, you will change your expectations, i.e., you will change your life.

2. Practice gratitude so your emotions will catch up with you attitude.

3. Don't just thank God for good things – thank Him because He is good.

4. Job praised God in misfortune – the bases for return blessings. "I came naked from my mother's womb, and I will be naked when I leave. The Lord gave me what I had, and the Lord has taken it away. Praise the name of the Lord!" (Job 1:21, *NLT*).

5. Praising God in hard times won't cost you anything, God will see and remember, but focusing on bad things and complaining and criticizing will always pull you down to their level.

6. Look beyond your circumstance to what you have, i.e., forgiveness, justification, accepted, eternal life.

7. Remember, God gives, and He forgives, so give thanks.

8. "If you haven't learned the language of gratitude, you are not on speaking terms with God."

9. Harold Vaughan went three-days with a *Gratitude of Thanksgiving* in prayer, vowing to not make a request or ask for anything for three days. "The longer I thanked God, the more I realized how fortunate I was."

10. "In everything give thanks" (1 Thess. 5:18). Does this mean thanking God for problems? Does Paul make any distinction between good days and bad days?

11. Always remember what you were before God found you and saved you.

12. If you spend your life looking for the dark . . . the mistakes . . . the sins . . . the people who hurt you . . . you will find them and lots more.

Slide 73 of 76

D. 7 GRATEFUL STEPS TO OVERCOME OBSTACLES AND EVIL

1. Pray. "Pray for them which despitefully use you" (Luke 6:28).

2. Do right. "Do to others as you would like them to do to you" (Luke 6:31).

Slide 74 of 76

3. Testimony. ". . . truly be acting as children of the Most High, for he is kind to those who are unthankful and wicked" (Luke 6:35, NLT).

4. Do good. "Recompense no one evil for evil" (Romans 12:14).

5. Forget. "average not yourselves" (Roman 12:19).

Slide 75 of 76

6. Give them to God. "I will pay them back, says the Lord" (Romans 12:19).

7. Conquer evil with good. "Overcome evil with good" (Romans 12:21).

Slide 76 of 76

PART FIVE

7 INDISPENSABLE WORDS
FOR EFFECTIVE PRAYER

ADDITIONAL RESOURCES

POWERPOINT SLIDES:

To purchase and download the PowerPoint Slides go to
https://www.norimediagroup.com/pages/elmer-towns

VIDEO:

To purchase available video by Dr. Towns go to
https://www.norimediagroup.com/pages/elmer-towns

ADD-ON CONTENT

To purchase additional products in this series go to
https://www.norimediagroup.com/pages/elmer-towns

RELATED BOOKS

Available at https://www.norimediagroup.com/pages/elmer-towns

Made in the USA
Columbia, SC
13 September 2024